A Brief History Of Lies
Daniel Nanavati

People do not believe lies because they have to, but because they want to.
(Malcolm Muggeridge)

A Brief History of Lies

A survey of a wicked, irreverent, serious, harmful, cruel and enjoyable (for some) side of human civilization.

Including quotes on lies and lying (good, bad and indifferent) from famous people down the ages who should know better.

By
Daniel Nanavati

with
Calvin Innes

Without lies humanity would perish of despair and boredom.
(Anatole France)

Each day a few more lies eat into the seed with which we are born, little institutional lies from the print of newspapers, the shock waves of television, and the sentimental cheats of the movie screen. (Norman Mailer)

Contents

Clever liars give details, but the cleverest don't.
(Anonymous)

Thank You

This book would not be what it is without the editorial assistance of Polly East, Jenna and Jackie Pascoe.

I would not be what I am without the help and assistance of my mother, Shänne Sands.

To the rulers of the state then, if to any, it belongs of right to use falsehood, to deceive either enemies or their own citizens, for the good of the state: and no one else may meddle with this privilege.
(Plato)

Preface

Why do we lie? The answer may seem obvious to you because you know why you have, and even when you haven't quite known the answer it was never important enough for you to fret over, especially when you got away with it. But in the very obviousness of the answer we all may be missing the deeper underlying reasons. In a very interesting conversation I had with the respected Oxford anthropologist Bruce Corrie, he touched upon the natural order of things (in terms of evolution) and how everything we create and do, is a reflection of Nature. What is the evolutionary advantage in being able to lie?

The answer to this also seems obvious until you ask yourself what the evolutionary advantage might be in lying to someone you love?

This short book looks at some of the most recent research done by psychologist, behaviorists, sociologists and security services and tries to shed some fascinating light upon the subject. Suggesting that lies go deeper than we ever expected before, because of our ability to lie to ourselves; and that what may have been a survival mechanism has not only come to be used inappropriately but for some becomes, if not a way-of-life, then the way life works.

It is always the best policy to speak the truth – unless, of course, you are an exceptionally good liar.
(H. L. Mencken)

I DON'T KNOW WHAT IT IS...
THERE'S JUST SOMETHING I DON'T TRUST ABOUT HIM!

Categories of Lies
or
Mangoes and Onions

Before psychologists created themselves, the only people who talked about lies were philosophers, when they discussed ethics, and religious people on their way to becoming saints.

Everyone who wrote and thought about lies quoted each other regularly over the centuries. St. Jerome from St. Origen, St. Origen from Plato, who quoted Socrates:

"If. . . falsehood is disgraceful and useless to God, to men it is sometimes useful, if only it is used as a stimulant or a medicine. . ." (Plato, third book of The Republic. Not my translation.)

Another saint, St.Augustine, devoted two whole treatises to the topic. 'On Lying' and twenty-seven years later 'Against Lies', and he identified eight kinds of lie:

Lies in religious teaching.
Lies that harm others and help no one.
Lies that harm others and help someone.
Lies told for the pleasure of lying.
Lies told to "please others during conversation".
Lies that harm no one yet help someone.
Lies that harm no one and save life.
Lies that harm no one and save someone's "purity".

And, after all, what is a lie? 'Tis but the truth in masquerade.
(Lord Byron)

This list was the first of many, many more and I have a suspicion that ideas of purity, in one form or another, underline much of the comment made about lies, liars and lying.

Surprisingly, psychologists have only been seriously analyzing lies and why we use them since the 1980s. They divide lies into many different categories and choose differing categories and place differing emphasis on their categories. Much like any of us they have a set of ideas about lies – which ones we should be angry about, which ones we feel we should expect, and which ones we will divorce over. We all know what lies are and we all frown on them to a certain degree, but we all find a regular use and excuse for them. For the most part this book is all about those uses. And you can criticise those uses as being abuses of the truth if you wish to, no one will mind and I can't hear you.

But I do wonder why the 1980s, the decade of rampant Thatcherite monetarism and glasnost (openness) brought about a deeper study of lies?

Here are some more categories, many of which Augustine did not think of, itemized by people who have thought a lot about lying (in the nicest sense) and, as far as I know, are still alive and have no ambitions to become saints:

Ambiguity:

> This is a deliberate attempt to mislead through the misuse of logic and the misuse of a talent for oratory. Syllogisms can be misused in this way. It is also a mainstay

A lie can run around the world before the truth can get its boots on.
(James G Watt)

of comedy, where we can recognise it instantly, but sometimes we fail to recognise it as lying elsewhere.

Bluff:

This is the pretence to possess a power or an intention which one does not actually have. Bluffing is an act of deception which is accepted and indeed expected as a tactic in games and every other walk of life. Poker and Blind-Man's-Bluff wouldn't exist without it. Neither would Hollywood.

Brazen:

A brazen lie is one which is told when it is obvious to the teller and to those listening, that it is an untruth. For example, a child who has chocolate all around his mouth who denies that he has eaten any chocolate is a brazen liar. In the present climate anyone saying, I am a trustworthy banker would also fit this category especially if the banker had chocolate around his mouth.

Conceit:

Lying to oneself. Certainly this is a clear case of misplaced compassion. Whole communities can lie to themselves.

Contextual:

These lies take the truth out of context

A lie told often enough becomes the truth.
(Lenin)

thereby making someone believe it isn't the truth. So saying sarcastically, "Oh sure! Your sister gets pregnant, and you go and blame me?" would fit this category if the speaker was responsible. Sarcasm is always a lie as it pretends to be either the height of intelligence or humor and is often neither.

Dissembling:

This implies presenting facts in a way that is literally true, but intentionally misleading. A debt collector offering, if you pay half your debt, to pay the other half would be dissembling (and desperate).

Emergency:

These lies are told in situations where harm may befall someone if that someone is told the truth. Years ago I knew an Irishman who was adopted and we found his birth certificate. Finding out the names of his parents when he was over 30, he said if he ever met his mother he would kill her. He would have been somewhat happier not to have known about his birth certificate. The truth can hurt.

Equivocate:

Falsehood is invariably the child of fear in one form or another.
(Alistair Crowley)

Pure and simple evasion of the truth, which is accepted in several walks of life and taught in a few more.

Exaggeration:

We are born free. True, but not to the extent usually suggested! People don't think this is a very serious lie in most cases but for myself, saying this is the best country in the world when you know about thirty countries are saying the same thing with some justice encourages ignorant nationalism. But what would I know?

Fabrication:

A fabrication is saying something without actually knowing whether or not it is true. I was told many years ago that Concorde, the first commercial supersonic passenger plane, had crashed one more time than on the official record and the last crash had been kept secret. The same man told me he had a super-computer in his attic. (There's one in every village.)

Fraud:

Criminal fraud occurs when the victim loses (has stolen) a valuable possession with (apparently) no benefit to themselves but this is actually an intentional deception However, in the legal world lies,

Good lies need a leavening of truth to make them palatable.
(William Mcilvanney)

dissembling and deceit exist on both sides of the spectrum and lying is part-and-parcel of every working moment.

Gender Specific:

Lies women tell men: "You're so big"; "This is my true hair color"; "The earth moved" etc. Lies men tell women: "I am not lost"; "That looks good on you"; "I am sterile,", "I don't need a condom" etc.

Hoax:

Anything that happens for April 1st reasons.

Institutional:

It was Ignatius Loyola who said that if the Church told him black was white then black was white. Loyola's words are a perfect example of the dangers of institutions trying to change reality for their own benefit. A will of iron is often prone to the world of self-deception.

Jargonese:

It has to be said that when the Law was all in Latin it militated against the general public who did not understand a word of it. It is the same today in India where the Law is in English. This lack of understanding is

Any fool can tell the truth, but it requires a man of some sense to know how to lie well.
(Samuel Butler)

devised to support those 'in-the-know' and extends to many spheres of activity beyond the Law. (Quite literally beyond the Law in some countries.)

Jest:

Usually seen as a joke, this is a form of teasing intended to be enjoyed by everyone within earshot. "England has the best cricketers" has quite different meanings when said in a Surrey pub as to when said in Mumbai.

Linguistic:

We don't only lie with words, but sometimes there is a deliberate methodology within grammar and syntax to confuse and blind. Oxymorons are a standard example (revolutionary government, wise human-being, etc).

Noble:

A noble lie would normally cause discord if it were uncovered, but it assists the community when it is given. It maintains law and order which helps the rulers. Sometimes also called Paternalistic Lie, but note the male attribution. Nowhere did I find a maternalistic lie defined. Maybe a maternalistic lie would be something like, "Of course he's your son".

Don't lie if you don't have to.
(Leo Szilard)

Omission:

A husband may tell his wife he was out at a store, which is true, but lie by omitting the fact that he also visited his mistress (presumably he went to the store to stock up on infidelity condoms which he doesn't need being sterile). In most cases, the person merely omits some part of what transpired. It may not be much of a lie, but some people would have you believe it's a sin.

Pathological:

According to recent studies people who exhibit this condition have brains incapable of differentiating between the truth and fiction because of the way their synapses are connecting in the front of their brains.

Perjury:

A crime. Making verifiably false statements on a material matter under oath or affirmation in a court of law, or in any of various sworn statements in writing.

Propaganda:

Information is always propagandist and contains bias but sometimes this bias is intended. Advertisements are an obvious example. Years ago a breakfast cereal ran

He who is not very strong in memory should not meddle with lying.
(Michel De Montaigne)

adverts challenging people to eat three portions in one go, masking the fact that for cost reasons the size of the portions was being reduced.

Relationship:
>See the chapter on relationships.

To Children:
>See the chapter on children.

Vindictive:
>These are aimed at harming someone, a group, organization or country. Whilst thought among the worst kind of lies, lies given to one's lover are considered worse, at least by the lover.

White:
>A white lie would cause no argument if it were found out. They avoid giving offence, such as complimenting something one finds unattractive. But be careful, a white lie in one culture may be perjury in another.

This list, though more informative than Augustine's is by no means extensive. There are far longer lists, but I think we can get the drift. Human beings can lie about anything, anytime in any situation to anyone for

I detest the man who hides one thing in the depth of his heart and speaks forth
another.
(Homer)

any reason.

It's a skill.

Mostly we should expect them (especially if we live in Argentina apparently).

GREAT IDEA JENKINS... THOSE BABIES ARE REALLY FLYING OFF THE SHELVES!

The lies we find hardest to take are not those which are just deliberate but those that are also vindictive and planned. But beware, we are all different and some people hate the innocent, off-the-cuff white lie just as much as the nasty, selfish one. Their emphasis is not so much on what kind of lie they are told, but on the absence of truth itself. Thankfully for us, though not for them, they are in a minority!

Dr. Leonard Saxe, a polygraph expert and professor of psychology at Brandeis University, observes,

The visionary lies to himself, the liar only to others.
(Franklin D. Roosevelt)

"Lying has long been a part of everyday life. We couldn't get through the day without being deceptive."

As psychologists delve deeper into the details of lying they are finding that lying is a surprisingly common and complex phenomenon. Hence all the lists.

Is lying really a condition of being human? In a 1996 study, Dr. Bella DePaulo, a visiting professor at the University of California, Santa Barbara and her colleagues had 147 people between the ages of 18 and 71 keep a diary of their lies over the course of a week. They didn't just trust them to know when they lied (would you?).

"We had a 90 minute session explaining the whole study to them, including how we defined lies. We also encouraged them to list the lie, if they were not sure it counted as a lie; then my coauthors and I read through them all to be sure they qualified."

Most people, she found, lie once or twice a day – almost as often as they snack from the refrigerator or brush their teeth. Both men and women in the community sample (excluding the college students) lie in approximately a fifth of their social exchanges lasting 10 or more minutes; over the course of a week they deceive about 30 percent of those with whom they interact one-on-one. Furthermore, some types of relationships, such as those between parents and teens, are virtual magnets for deception:

"College students lie to their mothers in one out of two conversations."

Someone who always has to lie discovers that every one of his lies is true.
(Elias Canetti)

The college students lied in one-third of their social interactions. It is interesting to note the difference and one wonders if college students lie a little else because their whole world is about facts, clarity and thoughtful opinion. De Paulo does not include pleasantries or polite equivocations such as "I'm fine, thanks" in the definition of what constitutes a lie.

Dr. Saxe points out that most of us receive conflicting messages about lying. Although we're socialized from the time we can speak to believe that it is always better to tell the truth, in reality society often encourages and rewards deception. Showing up late for an early morning meeting at work, it is best not to admit that you overslept.

"You're punished far more than you would be if you lie and say you were stuck in traffic, moreover, lying is integral to many occupations. Think how often we see lawyers constructing theories to support their client's case or reporters posing to get good stories."

Dr. Saxe believes that anyone under enough pressure, or given enough incentive, will lie.

"Lying is a function of social interaction. Lies are constructed/maintained to foster social interaction and, if we want to reduce the frequency of lies, we have to make it possible for people to tell the truth – particularly about foibles/negative behaviour."

As shown in a study published in the 'Journal of Personality and Social Psychology', Dr. DePaulo and Dr. Deborah A. Kashy, of Texas A&M University, frequent liars tend to be manipulative and Machiavellian, not to mention overly concerned with the impression they make on others. Liars. . .

Some truth there was, but dash'd and brew'd with lies, To please the fools, and puzzle all the wise.
(John Dryden)

". . .don't always fit the stereotype of caring only about themselves. Further research reveals that extroverted, sociable people are slightly more likely to lie, and that self-confidence and physical attractiveness have been linked to an individual's skill at lying when under pressure."

This last observation accords with the accepted belief that physical beauty impresses people and the more beautiful you are the more inclined people are to believe you.

We lie to each other to cover up the truth, or the fact that we don't know anything, or to make ourselves look better. When I was 9 I told my school friends I was a black belt in karate so they wouldn't bully me. This was a useless (and brazen) lie as everyone knew I was nothing of the sort. Useless lies are why we start lying at the age of 4 so that by the time we are 18 we know how to avoid making an obvious lie. Obvious lies are left behind with childhood toys, unless you meet with someone who has heard it all before and can see right through you!

Most adults don't set out to lie; it's a reflex action given the situation and the people they are interacting with. There are some people who will lie to anyone and those who just lie to you and me – but who would never think of lying to someone with the power to arrest them.

We do train some people to lie well and to everyone. Although we probably all have that aptitude it can certainly be enhanced. Generally they work for the CIA, etc., in the United Kingdom we have MI5, MI6 and probably an MI7 and MI8 though who will admit to organizations existing that are supposed to be invisible?

The sexes are pretty evenly divided on who are

Great talker, great liar.
(French Proverb)

the better liars. Ability is, in fact, not a gender issue. But here are some obvious liars I put before you, for you to consider:

- All the leaders of the world there have ever been, have lied, though they didn't lie all the time and didn't lie to everyone all the time. But whoever they were, are and will be, they lied and will lie. What makes them good leaders is their knowing just when to lie, about what, to whom and for how long and to always have a ready excuse if the lie is uncovered.
- Every crook that has ever lived or will ever live, lies. They never steal, kill, plot or plan. They are just like everyone else in the world except they got caught.
- Baron Münchausen reportedly told people that he had travelled to the Moon, ridden cannonballs, and escaped from a swamp by pulling himself out by his own hair. Münchausen Syndrome is a disorder in which someone feigns illness in order to get attention. Münchausen Syndrome By Proxy is a disorder in which a caregiver (usually the mother) fakes or induces illness in their child or in another person in their care in order to gain attention and sympathy. You have to be a really good liar to have disorders named after you.
- Children's book writers who make it seem there is a place where fairies, goblins, witches and orphans all live a merry-go-round happy-ever-after existence. What whoppers!
- Train timetable compilers.
- The rich, no wholly truthful person ever made millions from anything.
- Advertisers.

Nobody speaks the truth when there's something they must have.
(Elizabeth Bowen)

- Actors whose whole lives are taken up with pretending. (I am told 'pretend' is not lying. What do you think?)

I am certain you can think of many more.

And then with all this lying to others we must address the far more relevant and often harder to detect kind of lies. Those we tell ourselves. Because at the heart of believing others' lies is the hope, desire, wish that they were and are telling us the truth. Because in the world we would prefer to live in, what they say to us, would never be lies.

Lying to oneself is something we all do. "I am not really overweight"; "I can get there on time"; "I am really funny"; "I am the most handsome person in the world because my mother told me so".

Some self given lies get dangerous, but in the main it is just a way of making sure we don't get too upset at ageing. And it helps writers enormously because we can kid ourselves into believing anything we write is worth reading - it is also a great way for hack writers to consider themselves something better than they are. In addition it helps editors who all want to be good writers and so very rarely can be because they have to stop being editors first. We are habituated to self-given lies, a theme I shall return to.

For the most part it is not easy to recognise a really good liar which is why a great deal of time and effort has been expended on lie-detectors and considerable credence given to training observers to watch suspects for their lies.

It is not the aim of this little book to overview

For my part getting up seems not so easy by half as lying.
(Thomas Hood)

every situation in which people lie. I will limit it from now to a few places such as politics, business and war, and relationships because the same 'kinds' of lying crop up in every sphere of life. And I retread these well known areas that others have written reams about for two reasons. To look at how evolution works in these areas and to look at how lying to ourselves allows us to plug into 'universal' lies.

But first a question.

When does this habit of lying all start?

If one cannot invent a really convincing lie, it is often better to stick to the truth.
(Angela Thirkell)

In Children
or
Machiavellian Intelligence

Lying would appear to be part of everyone's life (some even make it a lifestyle) and it begins very young. Modern child psychologists tell us that people of average intelligence start to lie when they are about 4 years old, of higher intelligence when they are about 3 years old.

They term this commencement of lying in the young 'Machiavellian Intelligence'. Presumably because Niccolò Machiavelli has something of a reputation for promoting craftiness. In point of fact he was just being honest about power politics as he saw it in his time, and had he seen any leaders getting power, extending their boundaries and ruling their populations securely, by being honest, he would have promoted honesty.

Dr. Victoria Talwar, of Montreal's McGill University says that lying is related to intelligence. Presumably this is why so many of us think we marry idiots.

A child's ability to tell us the Emperor has no clothes on has long been an endearing facet in some children. They say it as they see it which is a facility we don't appreciate in adults (but more of that later).

However, lying is an advanced skill because we learn it. Much of lying is no more than habit. We don't learn how to tell the truth. Well some of us do!

When a child lies they actually know the truth

If you want to be thought a liar, always tell the truth.
(Logan Pearsall Smith)

so they know they are lying, they have put together a falsehood which is still based on the way the world around them works, and they have the self-belief that they can sell their lie to those they are lying to. Therefore, lying demands both 'advanced cognitive development' as well as 'social skills'. Which is a lot for a four year old let me tell you.

This isn't true of all lies, some are told because of fear and other emotions. But maybe the time, place and situation in which we tell our first ever lie – possibly long forgotten to us as we age – marks out our pattern of lying.

I could never lie to my mother and get away with it because she saw it written on my forehead every time.

Apparently honesty doesn't require the same abilities presumably because we don't care as much if people believe us or not when we tell the truth, but we do when we tell them a lie. I wonder if this is some kind of 'affirmation' exercise. Since we can be certain ourselves of the truth of the matter, we have a certainty that cannot be shaken. But since lies are set in sand we need to know they won't slip away from us, and the agreement (spoken or not) of those we lie to sets the lie in firm foundations in our minds. A lie accepted by others has a reality of its own. An affirmed lie like this has the strength of the truth.

If there were a branch of psychology called Machiavellian Logic that strand of thought would certainly fit into it. Basically we have to 'catch out' a liar, but we don't assume in our language that we have to 'catch' the truth at all. We assume lies are the exception, the deviation from the mean-point.

"It's a developmental milestone," Dr. Talwar has concluded. That is, it is learned from our surroundings

It is sometimes necessary to lie damnably in the interests of the nation.
(Hilaire Belloc)

and how we try to deal with them.

A test the psychologists did to fix on four as the age this milestone is reached went something like this. Developmental work was done with children up to the age of four to see if they could save the princess doll from the wicked witch. Most when asked outright where she was hiding told the adults straight away but by the age of four the kids started to point in places where she was not hiding so as to help save her. Bright kids lied a year earlier. Of course the really, really bright kids looked at the adults and said, "Let's stop pissing about with dolls and talk about police corruption".

Interestingly they don't say if some of the children refused to answer. Presumably you have to have a certain degree of bravery to stay silent and perhaps we don't develop that amount of courage for a few more years, or perhaps we lie at four on behalf of the princess as long as we don't have any adverse consequences to ourselves. At any rate it shows the possibility that lying and fear go hand-in-hand. We wouldn't want to be in the clutches of the wicked witch (until we cannot avoid it and start paying taxes) and we don't want the princess doll to fall into her clutches either.

It also proves bright people are better at lying than average people because they have one year's more practice. So wherever you find high intelligence you may well find first rate liars and if you don't, I think you've found integrity.

On a deeper level the child has empathized with the princess' plight and doesn't want anything bad to happen to her. It would seem from this that the first kind of lies we can tell, are based upon a child's growing idea

It is Homer who has chiefly taught other poets the art of telling lies skilfully.
(Aristotle)

of compassion. Maybe they can lie about where the doll is earlier but they don't actually 'care' about what happens to her before they are four or so. It would be interesting to know if the same response was found if they used a cow hiding from a farmer come to send it to the abattoir, and if it was found to be the same why that compassion disappears in most adults, whereas saving a princess (another human being) does not. This assumes that a child of three or four knows that a doll represents a real human being, or that the doll is in some way 'real' to them, which I think is a fair assumption.

Of course there is something in this example that is not learnt. The child is protecting the princess doll from a threat. In a world where threats abound this kind of response is both sensible and community orientated in that the child is protecting someone else which is what the child expects others to do for them. There may be a kind of symbiotic logic here in that we lie hoping someone would lie for us in the same situation. Lies in this case are almost an instinctive form of protection. As we shall see although many lies are to protect the individual there are others that one may assume anyone would use in the same situation, and so carry this variant form of community benefit with them.

Take another study. A number of two and three year-old children were seated in an empty room and told not to look at a toy placed on a table behind them. The researcher left and secretly watched the kids by video returning to the room a few minutes later. Ninety per cent of the children looked at the toy, and the majority, about 64%, tried to conceal their peeking. One-third lied outright, saying they did not peek, while the other third

It is easier to gather up a bag of loose feathers than to round up or head off a single lie.
(Anonymous)

didn't answer the question, pretending not to hear it, (bravery issues).

At this age, wishes and imagination often get in the way of what is real. Sometimes a three year old will start to tell a story, and you will hear it start to get out of hand as s/he adds bits and pieces to fit the growing or incomplete ideas in their head. Three year olds are generally poor liars because they fail to lie appropriately. They do not consider that their listener will actually think about either their statements or their intentions in making them. As a result, they tend to lie at the wrong time or place, or neglect to think about other important facts, such as covering their tracks to conceal the lies. The same kind of process appears in people lying on the hoof and trying to keep the lie going over a prolonged period of interrogation. It is a fact that throughout our lives we like our lies to be quick and easy. Said and dead. Except they never are.

By age four, children know the difference between telling the truth and lying – and they know it's wrong to lie. So, generally, they are truthful, and when they are not it's obvious. But they also become more proficient at lying because they're more cognitively capable of taking into account the listener's belief in their statement.

With children aged four to six, they found that the children were better at resisting the temptation to peek. But those who did look were more apt to lie about it. Videotapes showed another important difference in the older children: After they looked at the toy, they didn't look very happy. They did, however, change their facial expression once the researcher came back, they literally "put on a face". So at age six we are ready to play poker

It takes a wise man to handle a lie, a fool had better remain honest.
(Norman Douglas)

and become actors.

As one five year old said, "You should never tell a lie because the brains inside grown-ups' heads are so smart they always find out". Cute kid, s/he will be a lawyer.

A more sophisticated level of lying emerges between the ages of six and eight. Children can now understand something like, "John wants his mother to think he feels bad about his grandmother not coming to visit". At this stage, it's not just the content of the lie, but the motive or attitude of the speaker, that can be doubted as well.

Looking ahead to ages ten and eleven, most children become able liars. The big difference at this stage is that parents and teachers are no longer seduced by the sound of a child's voice, the innocent look on their face, or an outlandish alibi (now I know). This plays out in adults because a good looking person is more likely to encourage trust in their listeners or readers.

What reasons do we have, outside of child psychologists' experiments, for lying?

• Are we hoping we can all base our lives on the same assumptions? (One religion for the whole world!)
• Because we don't like people not believing what we believe?
• Because we feel foolish?
• Because we don't like trouble?
• Because we benefit socially and materially from them?
• Because we enjoy it?

All men are born truthful and die liars.
(Luc de Clapiers)

Whatever the answers once we have learned to lie, our understanding of the use and power of lies is obvious when they work. And we work on making them work. They go from being a skill, to being a tool.

Dr. John M. Grohol observes that this first lying in the young is not to be malicious, but rather it is children manipulating their environment. For environment read parents, other kids, teachers and especially grandmother who has the tastiest sweets but never visits.

This manipulation has a pay-off. When we lie we get away with something, we get satisfaction, we don't get punished, we don't get bullied and the witch doesn't get the princess. It is a game-play with a positive benefit to the liar if they succeed even though it's a negative activity.

This means good liars probably become mathematicians, which is the only other activity humans have found that gets a positive from a negative.

Actually, lying is thought to be an 'evolutionary psychological process' (something the species needs) because lying is even seen in apes who, in experiments, used sign language to "blame" something they did on another animal when they were confronted with their naughtiness. This might be stretching it a bit as we don't know the ape equivalent of owning up. They may never do it. Maybe we evolved to tell the truth from an animal that always lied. Who knows?

But children are not silly. They know when adults lie and copy them. And children are more adept at facial cues than adults because their continued existence depends on them knowing they are looking at someone who wants them to live. Not something all parents want

Every government is run by liars and nothing they say should be believed.
(I. F. Stone)

all the time. As Dr. Grohol says,

"the truth is, kids learn by modeling and learning from the behavior they see in their environment."

Starting young we eventually lie in about 1 in 5 social interactions. (Or 5 in 5 of sexual interactions.) It's a normal, everyday occurrence many of us take

I am a lie who always speaks the truth.
(Jean Cocteau)

for granted, but people who are honest and expect honesty in others are maddened by this fact and end up getting far less sex than the rest of us. Because of child psychologists we now know not to blame the little apes as its not their fault they lie – it makes complete sense in some situations to do so. You can now spend a lot of time differentiating between the types of lies we all tell, and which ones are thought to be de rigueur and which ones are thought to be plain awful.

Children will boast, claim things and tell stories as a form of power play with their peers. This natural form of lying becomes something much more serious because you learn one crucial fact; people believe lies. You learn the lies they won't accept and you learn the ones they will. If the child is father and mother to the adult, this is a very dangerous lesson. But then adults don't go around telling other adults that they have a new red fire-engine in their house with a real engine in it. No, with the adult mind comes the sophistication to lie about the big issues.

But let me be honest here, although the adult goes on to lie about different things, and in different situations, the basis of why they lie stays the same. They lie about things that matter to them or the people they are lying to. It is never worth lying about something no one really bothers or cares about. I mean. . .where's the fun?

Dr. Frances Stott, Professor of Child Development at the Erikson Institute in Chicago explains it this way as we grow older:

"Children will lie for many of the same reasons adults do:

He who permits himself to tell a lie once, finds it much easier to do it a second and a third time till at length it becomes habitual.
(Thomas Jefferson)

to avoid punishment, gain an advantage in a social interaction, protect against an unwanted consequence, and to boost self-esteem. Like adults, sometimes they lie to demonstrate power, to maintain privacy, or to protect a friend. When a child lies, they are essentially trying to change a situation, to reconstruct things the way they want them to be at the time. Planned, well-thought-out lies, are something adults seem to practice more readily than children."

When we hear different people saying different things about the same subject it may not be because they are actually lying, just that none of them actually knows the truth. If someone told someone 4,000 years ago the Earth was flat, we can't say they were lying; just that they were mistaken. After all, to all intents and purposes, it looked flat to them. Perception anticipates belief. Of course then belief takes over and shapes perception.

There eventually comes a realization that you won't always get away with a lie so there is a time and place for lying if you don't want to be known as a pathological liar or fantasist. Lies are not there to distance yourself from the community. Quite the opposite. Many are simply given to forestall an argument, for an 'easylife'.

As we grow we learn this. But parents share some blame because they teach lying. As much as the studies show there is an hereditary role, nurture cannot be forgotten. We can learn the worst habits very quickly when we are young and they are almost impossible to break. The relationship between the lies we learn and the ability to lie we inherit is probably comparable to xenophobia in its myriad forms. We are born with an

There is nothing so easy as by sheer volubility to deceive a common crowd or an uneducated congregation.
(St. Jerome)

ability to become attached to those around us and hence be wary of strangers, but we are taught to hate strangers and the strange.

Here are some of the peccadilloes we are taught, and which we pass on to our children without the slightest hesitation, in fact we believe them to be enjoyable lies. Even a normal part of childhood because they were part of our childhoods.

1. Adults' insistence that the Tooth Fairy, Santa Claus, Little People etc, exist is a pervasive lie in many, many cultures. Even when it isn't specifically these it is a bogey-man of some kind, a ghost of some kind, a mythical being of some kind. The origins of these beings vary according to legend and culture. Parents carry on insisting they exist for as long as the children will believe them as a part of the role play of childhood. When their non-existence is revealed it is the beginning of depression and a career in Hollywood writing Christmas feel-good films.

2. It is apparently difficult to talk to children about vaginas and penises. It's even difficult for children to think about their parents having vaginas and penises and it is a wonderful part of modern society that in some families at last, there is either no penis or no vagina. These families don't have to tell children about sex and birth, they can just tell their children they were chosen. The ones left who still have to tell their children about sex will invent things to stop from having to tell the sexual facts. Besides, storks and miracles are the way all women wish children came into the world, so it doesn't

In our country the lie has become not just a moral category but a pillar of the State.
(Alexander Solzhenitsyn)

actually seem to be lying more like wishful thinking.

3. All children have the beauty of babies, the wonder of toddlers, the handsomeness of growing up. But we don't leave it there. We tell them they are film stars. Which is a terrible thing to tell them when you see the disastrous lives film stars have. It's almost wishing them to unhappiness. Some children really are the most beautiful in the world. The rest of us will have to treasure the lies our parents told us. Some lies are worth treasuring.

4. We want our children to live forever. In fact we want to live forever but we will tell our children versions of 'you will live 100 years', knowing we have no idea whether or not it will be true. This is more wishful thinking and when the child is sick with cancer at 45 or for some other reason doesn't make 100, they won't blame their parents for lying to them, they will have long ago forgotten it.

5. Divorcing parents do, according to the psychologists, divorce their children from their parenting duties. It is never going to be quite the same again. Children are divorced from schools, and often homes and have new adults to contend with. The Children's Society report 2009 showed in the United Kingdom some 23% have stepfathers. And remember the children will have to live with this for 100 years, without the back up of Santa Claus and realize this is where sex leads the most beautiful adults in the world.

When lying, be emphatic and indignant, thus behaving like your children.
(William Feather)

The terrible thing about lying to children in this way is that they always find out the truth and then two things happen. On the one hand, they won't trust everything you say anymore. On the other they recall how comfortable, and lovely life was when they were living in the belief that the lies of the people who were looking after them and supposed to love them the most, were true. So they confuse love and lying, happiness and lying, ease of living and lying . . . you get the picture. Other children who see their parents lying to get on have an even worse world view.

And it goes on to pervade every facet of what we do. The rest of this little book is about adult lying. You know what adults are - the consequences of children.

I would dodge, not lie, in the national interest.
(Larry M Speakes)

In Adults
or
Dishonesty As Policy

Well obviously, adults learn to lie from watching their four year old children with child psychologists.

The other way they learn is from embarrassment, which is what clothes are for – if the Adam and Eve story is indicative of anything. That said, we should recognize all clothes are theatre and when they are not covering up our embarrassment, they are saying something to the world that we want the world to believe about us. Whether or not it is true. Maybe all lies are in some way saying the same kinds of thing. A mask that we think protects us.

As we have seen, until recently lying was not deeply studied by psychologists and those who did deal with it, being as we saw mostly ethicists or saints, saw it as a problem to be solved, a vice to be resisted, except in very rare and specific instances. Lying and ethics have a relationship because truth-telling and ethics have a relationship. Because human intellect has a relationship with ethics. Indeed, Ethics have become the defining characteristic of humanity.

However if lying is in any way an evolutionary development, if we think about it, there may actually be a point to lying and that evolutionary point may be the residual reason why we continue to lie so much despite our desire for truth and in contradiction to most ethical

In human relationships, kindness and lies are worth a thousand truths.
(Graham Greene)

thought.

Freud wrote a little about lying, and the Encyclopaedia of Psychology, published in 1984, mentions lies only in a brief entry about detecting them. Detection though, may be the real point of them!

Human beings have a particular penchant for believing in wonders. To know that when you were lied to was a very happy time of your life full of fairies, saints, fauns and magical worlds, leads one to wish to be lied to again in the hope of recapturing that rare experience of wonder mixed with warmth. Happiness and security. Which is a nice idea but what about people with insecure memories of childhood. Lies work in their lives too.

The ability to lie is obviously part of us, maybe dissemble would be a more acceptable word, but the question we have to ask is what caused that ability to exist in our brains in the first place and has it grown stronger for a reason?

The obvious answer is that dissembling can save life, yours or someone else's. There was a theory that fainting was part of our make-up because, rather like the possum, passing out and being inert in the face of danger (say a bear coming to find a meal) enhances survival rates by making us motionless in some non-specified undergrowth. In other words if you can't outrun a predator fainting may be your next best option. In the same way learning to camouflage not only our bodies but our intentions, aims and meaning, gives us an advantage if we feel our interests, and/or someone else's interests are in some kind of antagonism or danger. Wishing to spare someone pain is not an

All men are frauds. The only difference between them is that some admit it. I myself deny it.
(Jerome K. Jerome)

example of this, but business competitors lying to each other, would be.

Unusually for inherent abilities lying helps not just the liar but the lied-to as well. For if we are evolved to lie as a survival mechanism, we are all forewarned to expect lies from each other. This makes us evaluate people's 'true' intentions. This makes us ask, what advantage do they have in lying to us and what would they lose, if anything, if they told us the truth, in any given situation? This means that in a world of lies the astute and linguistically sophisticated, the story-teller and the realist, the crooked and the honest are in a continuous war with each other and in some ways this benefits the mind because we have to sort through a vast array of information to disinter the truth in the face of the many forms a lie can take. However it should be noted that continual lying of the kind we all encounter and give out, doesn't benefit society at all. There are those who argue lies of lesser kinds smooth over human relations, but actually we would all do much better to have the truth out in the open and not have to wait a century for the historians to uncover it.

The honest person who hates prevarication and tells it as it is, is usually a very unhappy person in today's world since they are in a minority. It is very difficult for them to deal with people who do not match their truthful outlook on situations, who dissemble and mask their true intentions towards them. This is especially true when they have to do any kind of business and interact on a professional level. We all know about the promises that are not kept. People who are used to lying and being lied to, do much better in organizations of all

A man would rather have a hundred lies told of him than one truth which he does not wish should be known.
(Samuel Johnson)

kinds than people who are honest. An honest person in today's society is really a round peg trying to fit into a square hole.

This is particularly interesting to me in the world of the arts where it is well known that modern movements entail a heady mixture of flattery, self-interest, hidden agendas and money to persuade other people of their merit and talent. Any individual artist meeting with these movements and adversely criticizing them, is rubbished, ignored and silenced through neglect of their own work. This happens across the board in almost every sphere of human activity and in every generation. It is the reason why many 'great artists' are picked up by succeeding generations and called 'ahead of their time'. They could have been just as popular in their lifetimes but they didn't play the lie game.

But some brains have taken lying to whole new regions of expertise. We call them pathological liars and until recently they were deeply denigrated as people who just lied and lied and lied. New studies show there is something far more interesting going on. So interesting that is the reason why 'evolutionary' actually is a pertinent description of some lying.

A recent study (2005) by the University of Southern California headed by Dr.Adrian Raine and Yaling Yang, has found the first potential proof of structural brain abnormalities in people who habitually lie, cheat and manipulate others.

Previous research shows that the prefrontal cortex (the area of the brain where we learn ethical behavior) is very active when normal people lie. Dr.

A little inaccuracy sometimes saves a lot of explanations.
(Saki)

Adrian Raine's team provided evidence that this area of the brain in pathological liars (those who cannot differentiate at all between truth and falsehood) is structurally different.

108 volunteers were recruited from the Los Angeles' temporary employment pool. A series of psychological tests and interviews placed 12 in the category of people who had a history of repeated lying (11 men, one woman); 16 who exhibited signs of antisocial personality disorder but not pathological lying (15 men, one woman); and 21 who were normal controls (15 men, six women).

"We looked for things like inconsistencies in their stories about occupation, education, crimes and family background. . . .Pathological liars can't always tell truth from falsehood and contradict themselves in an interview. They are manipulative and they admit they prey on people. They are very brazen in terms of their manner, but very cool when talking about this."

After they were categorized, the researchers used Magnetic Resonance Imaging to explore structural brain differences between the groups. The liars had significantly more "white matter" and slightly less "gray matter" than those they were measured against.

Specifically, liars had a 25.7 % increase in prefrontal white matter compared to the antisocial controls and a 22% increase compared to the normal controls. Liars had a 14.2 % decrease in prefrontal gray matter compared to normal controls.

Interestingly this isn't particularly seen as a deficiency problem, but more as an advantageous evolutionary shift.

Liars need to have good memories.
(Algernon Sidney)

"Lying takes a lot of effort. It's almost mind reading. You have to be able to understand the mind set of the other person. You also have to suppress your emotions or regulate them because you don't want to appear nervous. There's quite a lot to do there. You've got to suppress the truth. Our argument is that the more networking there is in the prefrontal cortex, the more the person has an upper hand in lying. Their verbal skills are higher. They've almost got a natural advantage. They've got the equipment to lie, and they don't have the disinhibition that the rest of us have in telling the big whoppers. . . .

When people make moral decisions, they are relying on the prefrontal cortex. When people ask normal people to make moral decisions, we see activation in the front of the brain. . . .

If these liars have a 14 percent reduction in gray matter, that means that they are less likely to care about moral issues or are less likely to be able to process moral issues. Having more gray matter would keep a check on these activities."

If these findings are replicated and built upon it could be of use to many different kinds of professional. Yaling Yang suggests, among other things, in the legal system they could potentially be used to help police work out which suspects are lying; in business they could assist in pre-employment screening, working out which individuals may not be suitable for hiring; and so forth. (So the new discrimination laws will not be about the color of your skin but the color mix of your prefrontal cortex!).

In their findings, the authors mention that separate studies of autistic children – who typically have trouble lying – have showed the converse pattern of gray matter/white matter ratios.

"The facts that autistic children have difficulty lying and also show reduced prefrontal white matter constitutes the opposite

Sometimes the lies you tell are less frightening than the loneliness you might feel if you stopped telling them.
(Brock Clarke)

STUART'S 'POKER-FACE' HAD LET HIM DOWN AGAIN.

but complementary pattern of the results compared to adults with increased prefrontal white matter who find it easy to lie. . . .

Although autism is a complex condition and cannot be taken as a model for lying, these results. . .converge with current findings on adult liars in suggesting that the prefrontal cortex is centrally involved in the capacity to lie."

(The other researchers were Susan Bihrle and Lori LaCasse, also of the USC College's psychology department, Patrick Colletti of the Keck School of Medicine of USC's department of radiology and Todd Lencz of Hillside Hospital's department of research.)

Although these findings are fascinating the samples are very small and some experts do not find them at all compelling.

Lies are sufficient to breed opinion, and opinion brings on substance.
(Francis Bacon)

Diana Fishbein, a behavioral neuroscientist at the Research Triangle Institute International in Raleigh-Durham, N.C[d1] has worked in

"an area of research about psychopathology in general and deception in particular. We are interested in what the neural substrates are for deception. It would be very interesting to know when someone is lying and how lying is manifested in the brain."

One of her studies found a major difference in the brain function of people who exhibited psychopathic behavior.

"Most people process higher-order cognitive function with the front of the brain and emotions in the limbic system, which is lower down. . . .Psychopaths treat emotional stimuli as if it was dry information, while cognitive information that includes rewards is processed in the limbic system."

The limbic system is a set of brain structures which support a variety of functions including emotion, behavior and long term memory.

The brain, which is the greatest processor of information in the known Universe, has evolved to lie in specified situations. For some people, as you may expect in an evolved system, this ability has gone too far in the face of our ethics. But it has implications for all of us as none of us will have the same white-matter/gray-matter ratio and research needs to be done to find out how the ratios play-out amongst the mass of us and if this 'ability' needs to inform us as we teach our children that fighting the wish to lie (in most cases) is the better course of action.

Lying is like alcoholism. You are always recovering.
(Steven Soderbergh)

But, whatever further research proves, the truly challenging aspect of our ability, and the differing abilities individuals have, to lie, is the way in which we can lie to ourselves with utter conviction.

At the other end of the scale from pathological liars, are people who hold as an absolute truth something which is just a belief and who consider others wrong to disagree with them.

All ideas have evolved. These evolved ideas have their own survival rates. These evolutions can be tracked and are usually quite logical. Many people around the world would say today that polytheists were mistaken. Even Hindus who are routinely 'accused' of being polytheists because it has come to be seen as something less than monotheism, explain that their idols are the many differing images of one god who has an unlimited number of images. And not a few Romans and Greeks throughout the Classical period thought as much of their pantheon of gods as atheists do today, but for the believers 'at the time' it was an unshakable truth. In fact it was a truth worth killing for, worth dying for and demanding a certain public fidelity. This is how we usually treat truths. We get very confused with our ethical systems and we will kill for what we believe is true, as readily as we will kill someone we believe is wrong! If aliens had to describe humanity based upon our history that would be their first finding. A willingness to kill.

The whole idea of heresy requires an orthodoxy, and orthodoxies are limited to times and places and cultures. Like fashion trends when seen by others looking back into history or from another part of the

Lying and stealing are next door neighbors.
(Arabian Proverb)

world, they look strange, foreign, sometimes laughable and almost at times unimaginable. Who today would consider anywhere in the world, burning a baby to death as a religious imperative?

At the root of defining what a lie is, we must accept that, because of the way the human mind works, the extent of human knowledge is a key factor in our judgment of what constitutes a lie. So today we know that there no spirits living in rivers, but they were not sure about that at the time when they believed in Naiads. (Some people are not sure they don't exist even today). It is, after all, very easy to see a willfulness in nature's capricious waywardness. Lightning as gods fighting, floods as punishments, deranged behavior as demonic-possession etc., when you don't have a wider knowledge to have a better or even a different theory as to what these things are and why they happen. Especially when these things can kill you and so possess a very strong fear factor for human beings. We are informed by the nature around us – parrot gods were not created in the West because there were no wild parrots there. But when you are taught these ideas from childhood as part of learning how the world works, they take on a whole different meaning. Not merely part of our ideas of the world but part of our ideas of ourselves. Just as we have seen lying to others starts very young so too does lying to ourselves. Lying to ourselves is the skill that truly gets us through the days of our lives.

When someone said the stars were holes in the firmament through which heaven's light shone and they knew they were just guessing, would that constitute a lie? Is a best guess a lie? Is a belief system a best-guess

Every violation of truth is not only a sort of suicide in the liar, but is a stab at the health of human society.
(Ralph Waldo Emerson)

game? Perhaps since we now know there is no life without a sun, sun worshippers had it right all along – except for the baby sacrifice debacle.

As far as we know monotheistic thought is about 3,000 – 5,000 years old. Since human beings have had the same size brain in excess of 150,000 years, it would be my guess that there being a single creative genius (one god) was possibly thought about long ago but we will never actually know. When human beings began to settle and write down their belief systems the most ancient stories they told were of gods, spirits and meta-beings of many sorts, not a single god. But if you look at the road from polytheism to monotheism and see it as an example of reductionism, you can see how this is obviously the development of thought since starting with one god and developing into polytheism, is not a logical process. There is beauty in unity; not that outside of poetry, beauty is a good reason for believing anything. But merely that logic does have a definable beauty in its ability to describe great things in simple terms, and one god is obviously going to be a supremely powerful being, and supreme power appeals to the human gift for creatively designing unanswerable authority into our belief systems. We mirror it in our insistence in having one political leader at a time.

Belief systems are great stories but we all know stories are just that, stories – fictions to greater or lesser degrees. They are all based on fact – even the weird and wonderful world of children's writing in which I live doesn't have many fictional beings that are not in some way based on what 'living beings' are like. This 'fiction' nonetheless manages to exhibit lessons in truthfulness.

> You can fool too many of the people too much of the time.
> (James Thurber)

Because as we find out more about the world we tend to leave behind mistaken ideas and thoughts - those ideas are still in our history and mutate and still have a life with some people, but in the main ideas move our lying and our truthfulness on to new avenues. In this way lying and truthfulness are like a drama acted on the stage of the human brain. And who knows how many acts we still have to sit through. I doubt though many people would want to believe that belief systems exist because lies do, but it is interesting how we loop our ethics around our belief systems in a symbiotic relationship that we believe to be exclusive, but actually is not. It is possible to be highly ethical and not have a religion at all. It may even be preferable as having no god gives one supreme responsibility, as there are no get-out clauses of any nature.

There are many different explanations in belief systems about how the world was created. They cannot all be correct. But is it a lie to believe something to be true that isn't? Or is it just misguided? And given the fact that human beings are the most untrustworthy creatures on Earth is believing someone is watching you all the time not a sensible fiction to have people believe in? If CCTV cameras have lessened crime an all-seeing god must have some beneficial effect!

It is a shame that some sects believe they are 'right' and other belief systems are 'wrong'. To believe something that is only proven to yourself and to decry other people the right to prove things to themselves that are different, seems misguidedly selfish, even if it is very human. But it is a very human result of lying to oneself.

If there is a god he's been playing hide-and-

Sometimes I lie awake at night, and ask, Where have I gone wrong? Then a voice says to me, This is going to take more than one night.
(Charles M. Schulz)

seek for the thousands of years human beings were ardent polytheists, and it's no fault of human beings if they think there are millions of him/her/it. The lies and counter lies in which people partake are part of the mixture of belief systems because some parts of all belief systems no matter how divinely inspired their believers say they started, are human creations. And, as we now know, human's have the ability to lie about anything if they can derive great comfort or get some 'handle-on-the-unknown', by doing so. Especially if they have reason to fear the unknown – after all would a powerless god who cannot look after all of us be one we would even want to believe in? What would be the point?

The addition to our beliefs about god, of ethical teaching (seen by some as the whole point of having a belief system) can only be because people lie to each other. As these belief systems see it, we need to tell each other the truth more. The whole idea that belief systems teach 'how to live' can only be because without them the founders of these belief systems were not that impressed by how people were living. In fact, deep in our subconscious selves, we may one day find that belief systems are a very human answer to the very human problem of the prevalence of lies. But then again. . .we may not.

Self deceit (as we touched on above) gives one a system within which one can live in a sense of happiness. No matter what is happening in the world, that there is a god in some kind of overall control can be placed in this context. It is an engine for a certain kind of happiness or contentment. Much of religiosity

No one can lie, no one can hide anything, when he looks directly into someone's eyes.
(Paulo Coelho)

(the structure, hierarchies and daily workings) of belief systems are designed to promote this contentment. To cement one's adherence and focus the mind. Which is why dissent and doubt are seen as enemies. Indeed heresies. And there can be no greater dissent than another belief system with its own structure and hierarchies.

It's part of the process of going back to that time as a child when someone else puts the food on the table, puts the table in the house, puts the house in the street.
..

Isn't it strange that a lie (known or unknown) can actually provide a form of happiness? And maybe we lie a lot more than we need to or should, because we are striving for those moments of happiness. Our belief systems have evolved along with us, as have our science, our ethics, our languages and everything about our thinking. And it should be expected that they would. For the whole of nature is about surviving and every religion since the dawn of our minds has had something to say about death. Why? Because it is the one thing we know we cannot survive. In the face of this, reason evolved belief systems, which have in them arguments for survival after death in one form or another. We appreciate embalming for the same reason, because it is easier to believe in a continued existence for our personalities if the body is more or less looking like it did when we lived. It is far harder to believe anything survives when grubs eat away the flesh and skeletons rot down. Hence the creation of the idea of a soul, because belief-systems have always been explanations of our experiences when we have had no other explanations to

The lie is the basic building block of good manners. That may seem mildly shocking to a moralist – but then what isn't?
(Quentin Crisp)

turn to. The soul being felt not seen, does not die.

But as Spinoza so brilliantly observed our 'experience' is wholly based in, on and around nature. We know nothing that is not of nature and we cannot describe any god or gods without reference at all stages to nature. Therefore to all intents-and-purposes god and nature are one-and-the-same. Our belief systems are deeply entrenched attempts to escape this fact.

As we have surveyed forms of lies and touched upon the evolution of lying and what they could be used for outside of their immediate purpose, I shall spend the rest of this book looking at specific areas of lying: politics, business and war, and relationships. That is if you haven't burned it!

There are many other spheres I could have chosen as in medicine, farming, law,etc. but for the most part the forms of lies never change from sphere to sphere and my choices are more than enough to give you adequate food for thought. Finally I will itemise research on how to recognise when someone is lying.

No man lies so boldly as the man who is indignant.
(Friedrich Nietzsche)

In Politics

or

Evasion, Concision, Position

Machiavelli had it right. You have to be able to lie, kill and hurt without conscience in the short term, to be a leader capable of making millions or people you don't like do something they don't want to do. In fact he remained right up to 1939. After the Second World War leaders finally realized there is a 'community charge' we all pay for their lying on our behalf. But there are still many leaders today who seem to think they just have to sell you a story to maintain rule over you. And if their aim is to maintain rule, they are right because their authority rests upon a brilliance at population control (in its non-breeding connotation). I rather like the ex-Labour Member of the British Parliament, Tony Benn's adage 'I don't want to be ruled by anyone who wants to rule me.'

But one party states or dictators are not alone in their lies or in having a methodology upon which they base their lying. Knowing when to lie, to whom and for how long is one of the arts of politics. Actually, its probably become one of the arts of all and every career.

Although many of us have a democratic system which has taken thousands of years to develop, these days this system does seem to work on the basis I would describe as short-term dictatorships. Parties with fewer votes than another party can rule, parties in power have

The naked truth is always better than the best dressed lie.
(Ann Landers)

veto rights and can, and do, steamroller legislation through Parliaments.

Most political parties will lie about their true intentions when trying to gain power, and all do things once in power they specifically have said they would never do when on the hustings (raising taxes being the most common). We, the voters, let it go thinking we have pressure groups that bring these things to our attention and liberty groups to make enough noise when we need waking up. But in the main we seem to accept that if we take against a party, voting it out of power at the next election is punishment enough. This has naturally grown a sense amongst the political elites that elections are a form of sanction and they take it as part of the ups and downs of political life that they will lose power once in a while. So being in the opposition becomes as much of a power play as being in control. The only thing they really get upset about, are new parties threatening their power bases or, horror-of-horrors, making the voting system more democratic by making it proportionally representative.

This cosseted idea of politics leads intellectually different parties to do many of the same things in the wider political sphere. Parties will hide legislation in the small print, try to get away from bad news quickly and let good news out early to make the most of it. They bask in success and blame others for failure. They quell dissent in their ranks, retire difficult officials, buy off people they cannot get rid of who disagree with them (this is euphemistically called compromise), leak against people in their own parties who are 'rivals' (how can you be a rival if you all represent the people?), and a myriad

One of the striking differences between a cat and a lie is that the cat has only nine lives.
(Mark Twain)

other dubious activities none of which act in favour of either the electorate or the country.

Most important of all they ride tides of popularism attempting to dress themselves in the clothes everyone wants them to wear whilst underneath remaining just the same. (The best liars always seem to have a smile on their two-faces.) Have you ever wondered why parties are so similar? Your vote made them so. In fact leadership of any kind breeds lies because those who are led ask so many questions the leaders can never have well constructed answers to them all and if they tell the truth the led will lose confidence in them. Lies maintain the people's confidence and the people who are lied to, in the main, prefer to keep their confidence over being told the truth. We are back, at this point, to where lies give us a more comfortable view of life and, as far as I can see, this is the only reason for anyone to allow political lies to go unchallenged. For a political lie is a corruption and corruption unchallenged will only ever get worse.

Fundamental shifts come rarely and usually in an upheaval within the community. An upheaval so stark they are often termed revolutions even when not bloody. Politics is all about the status-quo because that is the path of peace and prosperity. But since prosperity itself relies upon an economic system that must always grow within a finite resource (the planet Earth) it is itself 'a fools' paradise' , even if those fools will be our great grandchildren and even if the crisis it will bring has taken thousands of years to come about. The system in which we are living and the planet Earth are on a collision course and no one will admit it. It would dent

We lie loudest when we lie to ourselves.
(Eric Hoffer)

our confidence.

Politicians are able to lie to us because we lie to ourselves. Jobs are not as important as breathing, anything that harms breathing must be stopped. But as long as only a few living creatures and a few fellow citizens stop breathing because of our prosperity, that appears to be OK. Risk is a description of acceptable losses, not an ethical proposal. To lose one species on our watch would seem to be a misfortune, to lose thousands has to be deliberate carelessness. We would rather watch mass extinction than admit economics is a bad system upon which to base civilization.

Most of this tendency to lying, opacity and prevarication from leaders comes from the fact that no individual has 200 years to put anything right, we

IT SAYS HERE YOU SPENT TWO YEARS AS THE
SUPREME MASTER OF THE UNIVERSE?

Oh, what lies there are in kisses.
(Heinrich Heine)

only have one lifetime and in democracies we don't even have that long, we have a legislative period of time between elections. This kind of pressure forces people to lie just to be able to get anything at all done. Filibustering takes many shapes and forms and long term planning is not structured into our systems.

How could one even begin to put generational changes into such a short term system? Well, we could begin by not allowing politicians to lie about it or we could demand long term agreements between parties before we elect them. We could create online forums to tell them what we want them to do and not wait for them to generate their own manifestos. Fundamental to this would be the consensus for the first time in human history, that stewardship of nature and not economics is the most important factor in politics. And the names of the leaders are meaningless. But we like economics. We like money. Its an extension of how we think and we are not evolved enough to do without it yet. Until of course, there is a stark upheaval. But even if one were on the horizon, for the sake of the status quo our politicians would never tell us. If they can get through their few years of power, they know they can spend the rest of their lives blaming everyone else.

The task of leadership requires the leader, according to Machiavelli, to be publicly above reproach, but in private it may require immoral things to be done in order to achieve their goals. 'Their' goals, not the people's goals.

In other words politics is the art of the hidden lie. Or as politicians term it – evasion or secrecy for the public good. Politicians have been lying like the rest

No man has a good enough memory to make a successful liar.
(Abraham Lincoln)

of us since the age of four and 'negotiation' (the sine qua none of politics) is dependent on an intellectual play that drips out the truth slowly, if at all. Politicians are simply not being trained to be truthful and the structures into which they place themselves (political parties) are not inherently honest structures. How could they be? They have been created by a bunch of lying human beings.

Someone said when the Tory Party was created in the United Kingdom in the 1670s,

> "A political party is little more than a conspiracy against the rest of the nation." (Quoted by C V Wedgewood: The King's War).

Excellent historian though she is, this quote is unattributed, but it is far too true across the world to be ignored. A politician's lie is a personal conspiracy. But maybe every lie is an individual's personal conspiracy against those they are lying to.

Some people argue that a politician who has an affair should not lose their status because it's only sex. If that politician has an open relationship with their spouse I would agree with this, but if their spouse was lied to then it is correct that politicians should be brought to account. How can you even try to trust someone who lies to those closest to them? If they can lie to their spouse (whom they are supposed to 'love') they can lie to anyone. If they can betray oaths given in public (marriage) their word is proven to be untrustworthy. It is, after all, one thing to know we are being lied to and quite another to catch out the liar. Although four out of five lies goes unnoticed and shouting about the one we

A liar begins with making falsehood appear like truth, and ends with making truth itself appear like falsehood.
(William Shenstone)

do notice might be considered ludicrous, to the political classes it is usually considered no more than bad luck.

There are many, many assumptions we have grown up with over the generations that were begun by people without our depth of knowledge. A country cannot be said to lie, but have you ever seriously thought of why we have countries, and is the existence of countries consistent with human behavior which we have now seen is a behavior that is 20% liar?

There were no countries before human beings came along. As we would assume everything we make reflects how we think and who we are, how far does the existence of countries reflect how we lie? Tribes fighting over their patch, languages which are basically different sounding noises referencing talk about the same things with a variety of idioms, have become gatherings of people all middling along in specific land-areas. I have the honor to live in a country that has created most of the countries on this planet because we had an Empire. Drawing maps was big business in the British Empire and redrawing them even bigger. So was breaking treaties because you cannot make an Empire without a lot of lying.

Of course legally countries exist – they have charters and sign agreements and peace treaties and set up border controls. We construct around us something we can get a handle on in our reason because the Earth is too big an idea to be contained in the intellect of past leaders. Countries are part of the cultured lie we tell ourselves because they are the wall over which we are able to view other people. But actually, philosophically countries don't exist at all. That isn't saying much I

Pain forces even the innocent to lie.
(Publius Syrus)

agree, as philosophically nothing exists.

But it may explain why saying, God Bless America, doesn't actually work because God doesn't actually know what you are talking about. (This isn't an American bashing book, I just liked the subtle complexity of the joke.)

The sadness of the human construct of country is that countries will work against each other and there is no common thread anywhere in history where the human race has ever acted as one race nor will there be until we stop lying so much. Countries are a perfect vehicle to promote lies and give human beings, with already restricted vision, a cubicle all of their own. Whatever will these thinkers do when the Universe opens up to the human race? Plant flags everywhere?

Politicians have a simple problem. They want to be elected into power again and again. They can't tell people that it's an ego trip because the halls of power are a heady mix of moment and authority, so they tell them the 'country' needs them, that they are a safe pair of hands and that they know what they are doing for the 'country'. Funnily enough, the people believe them, so they keep saying the same things generation after generation. The country as a political construct has been with us for so long we can no longer define ourselves in any other terms. We even have passports which is the perfect way for others to control their view of who we are.

If Pericles walked into the world today he would understand the lies the politicians were peddling. He invented a lot of them. (But he would be appalled at the mess the Greeks have made of the Parthenon).

So near is falsehood to truth that a wise man would do well not to trust himself on the narrow edge.
(Marcus T. Cicero)

Of course lying to your own people is one thing, lying to other countries is de rigueur. Sir Henry Wotton said that an ambassador is an honest man sent to lie abroad for the good of his country (or, as he said it, in Latin – legatus est probus homo ad alias nationes missus ut mentiatur pro suae rei publicae bono).

Double-entendre's like this are a way of dangling a truth in front of a person without actually revealing it, and making them smile if they get it and annoyed if they do not.

The real problem seems to be that no matter what the subject, no matter what the time, human beings cannot agree about anything, which is why in a democracy there is not just one party,anyway. We all have our own agenda, and in that lies the cause of many of our lies. Because politicians feel they are right. We lie because we are right (but we don't want others to know it yet). This is why we have something termed plausible deniability, and why it is impossible to get politicians to give straight answers. They know that in their place, we would be lying too.

John Arbuthnot (a satirist and well known wit) writing in England in 1712, concluded that the people should be frightened by the French King at least once a year to keep them on message. Something the modern British press has taken on board with gusto. The history of Europe has been a history of Empire building, and competing Empires always lie about each other. Lies to them are a useful weapon in the wider geo-political war.

Arbuthnot gives rules for political lying:

• They should be within the realms of probability

The liar's punishment is not in the least that he is not believed, but that he cannot believe anyone else.
(George Bernard Shaw)

(even a four year old knows that)

 • They should be varied (people who believe your small lies may well believe your big ones)

 • One should not obstinately insist upon a single lie (the more you repeat a lie the more likely it is it will be discovered)

 • Lies which promise or foretell something should not be repeated because they will be uncovered and speedily contradicted. (Brackets are mine)

In fact if you want to be a great satirist and wit too, sit down and work out which of your political parties are the greatest liars, when, why and how they have lied. It's a bit like shooting-fish-in-a-barrel but it has its moments. The art of political lying is actually a game. (Arbuthnot and Swift published the tract The Art Of Political Lying, they had an alternative title in Greek which I won't bore you with.)

The game is easy. Take two players or more. Give them power. Tell them one of them has power over the other every four years. Put in a wild card player who has to ask them questions all the time (we call this player a journalist) and mark them on the inventiveness of their lies. The serious side to this game is that people get hurt. Politicians get people killed and destroy lives with their policies, (and note in English 'lies' is part of the word policies). But remember that is part of the acceptable 'risk'. There will always be losers and as long as their numbers are manageable it is acceptable. The political agenda is all that is truly important.

So, politicians lie to stop people knowing everything they are up to. Sometimes they say they do

Lying rides upon debt's back.
(Benjamin Franklin)

this because it's a question of national security, but the nation is only a human artifice. Nature really doesn't recognise countries and now sadly in a mirror image of nature, politicians no longer recognise lies. If they can give an excuse for it, it isn't a lie. The 'greater good' is the most prevalent excuse. For the greater good, their default position is to increase their powers of control over the entire population. Increase it until you are perfectly safe from the threats from everyone – except your own politicians.

But we are also to blame here. We like being lied to. We like being told taxes are not going to be put up. We like being told cheap labour is destroying our workforce. We like being told we can drive whatever we want, kill whatever we want, buy whatever we want. Lies pander to our selfishness and our world view. The view from our 'country.'

The truth, that the world is finite and we have to have discipline and we cannot have everything we want just because we have buying power – reminds us of school. But politics is like a huge school. Our politicians teach us mathematics, economics and history. Every four years (or seven if you are French) they test our knowledge. When we elect them, we pass the test.

Jean-Michel Rabaté, Vartan Gregorian Professor in the Humanities University of Pennsylvania, published The Ethic of the Lie (2008). His focus is the American political scene but he points out:

"It is not that lying is more frequent in the United States than elsewhere, but, since the end of the Cold War, American culture has been polarized by this topic, finding in it an unlimited

There is nothing in the world more shameful than establishing one's self on lies and fables.
(Johann Wolfgang Von Goethe)

source of fascination, amusement, and horror. . . .We lie quite often, four to six times a day on average. . .at the same time, we do hate liars, and even more detest being lied to."

It is a curious factor of human thinking that we lie to ourselves in order to bolster our personal world view. And I suppose we lie to others to support that same world view. It is a curious arrangement lies have with self-affirmation and even our self-confidence. I am sure those who think about the theories of mind recognise

By a lie, a man...annihilates his dignity as a man.
(Immanuel Kant)

this very well.

We accept lies in politics in much the same way as we accept them in every walk of life. Much as money is the oil on which civilization runs, lies seem to be the treacle we all wade through when dealing with other people except for the fact we don't go around licking them all.

Ok that analogy didn't work.

Mostly politicians lie because they couldn't get much done if they told the truth. It would be too difficult because the opposition parties would be able to shoot them down all the time. Politicians lie to each other and about each other. Presentation is everything. After all, when a politician lies if other politicians can't prove it's a lie, then why should we be bothered? It will all change in four years anyway. In fact there is only one political party anywhere in the world and we should just vote the Liars Party in.

There is a school of political thought that says the best politicians are those who do the things the people want them to do, but make the people think it is they, the politicians, who thought of it. I am actually a fan of the psychological approach to history but in the context of the present discussion, this would mean that it is our individual aims and objectives that successful politicians are matching. Look around the world, this is the sum of your ambitions.

And whatever happens, don't blame me. I didn't vote for them.

Lies are essential to humanity. They are perhaps as important as the pursuit of pleasure and moreover are dictated by that pursuit.
(Marcel Proust)

In Relationships
or
If I Rip Your Heart Out Will It Hurt?

This will be the first chapter everyone reads (not). Oh what a tangled web we weave with all this practice to conceive.

Women all know men lie to try to have sex with them. Men all know women lie to get out of having sex with them. This means that the best relationships are those where most lies mostly don't work but the sex is still good enough for no one to mind much. Having sex with three or more people doesn't change this truth. And yet. . .and yet. . .how we yearn for truth.

If our lying is part of evolution, is it lying to get sex (and how good you are at lying to get sex) that dictates how well your genes are passed on? According to popular wisdom, women are more attuned to reading human character than men, so if liars have done so well at breeding, to the extent that we are all to greater or lesser degrees now liars, is it because women have been choosing liars to mate with for a long, long time? (Incidentally my aunt tells me, there is not a lot of choice!)

Has lying had such a positive effect on mating or is lying just a part of who everyone is anyway, and it has made no difference to the make-up of the human race as we are all 'born liars'?

There probably never was a time our ancestors

When a man lies, he murders some part of the world.
(Merlin)

didn't lie at all. Perhaps the truth is it isn't that important. If in our ancestry we chose to lie to get sex it was a choice made so long ago that it is irrecoverable what started it, but why do we still lie in every other walk of modern life?

Possibly because if there is an evolutionary element in it, it worked. On the other hand, like all good things, we can never leave well alone. We always expand on them and use them in inappropriate areas. It may be ok to lie to get sex, but once we marry, and make a commitment, it is no longer appropriate at all to lie either to the person we are married to or to the others we are not. People can accept small lies when they are dating but they are far less forgiving when it comes to commitment. With commitment a higher degree of honesty is supposed to arise. Why? If this expectation is also evolutionary what is its purpose?

Possibly the answer lies in the fact that we lie when we are unsure of someone or some situation, and it is only through familiarity that there naturally arises some measure of trust. Or maybe it is through familiarity that we derive some measure of trust in the lies we give and receive?

In the research on pathological liars and autism we have seen a potential correlation between mendacity and the make-up of the pre-frontal cortex. Since we may assume no one has exactly the same ratio of white and gray matter, we may assume many of us are at differing places on the ladder between only telling the whole truth and not recognizing the difference between truth and lies. We all have slightly different tendencies in this regard which may be exacerbated or blunted through

You don't tell deliberate lies, but sometimes you have to be evasive.
(Margaret Thatcher)

habits taught from childhood.

It is reassuring to think that mating has all been about avoiding the pathological extreme. If we were all pathological liars civilization would be untenable.

Much to the chagrin of popular literature and magazines all over the world, the truth is we lie, and whether it is for dating or for power, the reasons are much the same. We lie to gain advantage and it is gaining advantage that is the evolutionary bit of the puzzle. Lying to get sex is just an offshoot of our ability to lie. The continuation of our lies in the face of what we call 'ethical' behavior is probably because our ability to lie runs to the depths of self-preservation and selfishness. Both of which live at the level of instinct. A place where ethical behavior for all our high talk, does not live.

The fact is that telling the truth must be on the same level as lying, in that it too is part of our evolution. Even if it is an evolution of thoughts and ideas. But the difference is hidden in that word 'telling'. You don't need a language to lie, gestures and expressions can lie, so all the abilities, wishes, desires and uncertainties that lead us to lie, and conversely all the similar feelings that lead us to tell the truth, were probably part of us even before we learned to voice them. So it may be there are two abilities in contention within human evolution – at war with each other. One on the level of instinct and one on the level of reason. (That should satisfy the religious horrified by this talk of lying being hereditary).

Sex in-and-of-itself is also a kind of lie. It makes people believe they are in love, it makes people make decisions in order just to get the sex, it takes up most

Truth will lose its credit, if delivered by a person that has none.
(Bishop Robert South)

of our fantasy time, and it puts people into the most ludicrous physical positions – sometimes in public. And its aim is not the orgasm, its aim is the baby. The orgasm and desire are the things it uses to lead us by the nose. Literally in some cases. Sex is nature's greatest joke. And it's all ruled by hormones. If we could hear them I bet even beetles are laughing about it. The feel good factor in sex is so strong in some of us, it plays out in our lives just like a drug. And we go to enormous lengths to increase the feel good factor with an array of add-ons and plug-ins software manufacturers can only envy.

Is all attraction a form of lying? Well no, we can be attracted to someone's personality, we can be attracted to someone's mind but physical attraction yearns for sex. In other words if we find someone attractive, nature is saying, 'potential baby' – but we are saying, 'I might get lucky'. Nature and human beings really need to talk more.

Sexual desire is gender oriented – we sexually desire members of one sex or the other – but romantic attraction is personality oriented. We fall in love with a particular person, not their gender.

"Greater attention to processes of affectional bonding may significantly advance our understanding of how and why individuals show such diverse patterns of desire, infatuation, and love for same-gender and other-gender partners over their lifetimes."
(Lisa Diamond, 'What Does Sexual Orientation Orient? A Biobehavioral Model Distinguishing Romantic Love and Sexual Desire. The Psychological Review 2003)

There is a good deal written about infidelity and

With lies you may go ahead in the world, but you can never go back.
(Russian Proverb)

lying within relationships. More than there is written about political or any other area of lying. It's as if for some people it takes finding out someone has lied to them to make them curious as to why and because we all lie, there are a lot of these people around and many ready to give them answers.

We should expect lies. We should not act as if 'love' is supposed to bleach out all desire or opportunity to lie and yet, as commentators have said many times, out of an act of love (for someone else's benefit) is about the only time lying is truly permissible. What people actually seem scared about is not 'detecting' lies in those closest to them. To be lied to and not know it, makes one feel foolish, angry and used.

Many years ago I had occasion to ask a neighbor about something which to my face she flatly denied ever happened. Her daughter of fourteen was standing next to her as she lied to me. Her daughter grew up to lie to her and she was surprised at this. It is a sad fact that some liars expect to be told the truth. We all lie and sometimes those closest to us will lie to us. It is whether we hold those lies (if we recognize them) to be about important or non-important things that should guide us, not the fact of the lie.

Add to this, spouses who are in competition with each other for time with their children or even career prospects and the stresses and strains become even more apparent and lies flow that much more easily. The only good thing to be said about these kinds of lies is that they are not designed to hurt. Quite the opposite. Liars who set out to deliberately hurt those they 'love' are abusive and in need of medical help. But even

Do not think you are going to conceal thoughts by concealing evidence that they ever existed.
(Dwight D. Eisenhower)

those of us who routinely lie to those we love, should recognize that we have no powers to know whether or not those lies are hurting. They may well know we are lying. Maybe they are waiting for us to grow up. Maybe they have given up on us being truthful.

Sadly we should know that some people accept even the lies they know to be lies, even though it pains them deeply. In relationships the liar who thinks their lies have worked yet haven't, is the cause of immense suffering. Quite the opposite of the effect the lies are meant to be having. Quite the opposite of the general effect one would want in a committed, close relationship. We don't live with each other to be unhappy.

We must remember that love isn't something that exists of itself outside of individual human beings, it is generated in us and we are capable liars. It's going to be part of the mix. Even if we make judgments about the extent and quality of the lies we tell those closest to us, and even if we judge them benign, simple, unimportant, only of the moment – we are still lying. Thinking it over doesn't actually make any difference.

This is not about control issues which are frequent in dysfunctional relationships. Nor about lies that one person thinks important and the other doesn't. When I was five we lived next door a darling, elderly lady who worried a great deal about anyone mentioning the First World War, because she had lied to her husband throughout their marriage about her age and did not want to be caught out with memories he didn't think she could have! Personally I don't think Reginald would have minded finding out she was ten years older than she claimed but she never told him and in point

Lying to ourselves is more deeply ingrained than lying to others.
(Fyodor Dostoevski)

of fact as far as I know, he never asked. She admitted this only after he was dead to my mother as a woman-to-woman thing.

Does it matter if someone has had plastic surgery and doesn't tell their new love? Or hides the fact they have distant family in prison? Or conceals their wealth so they know the person wants them for who they are not what they can buy? When you look at the list below of things about which lovers lie (and remember it's not a detailed list), you are the only one who can judge their importance to you.

Sometimes though, as with our elderly neighbor, we share the lies we tell with some confidante. Is this because we are basically honest or because we are riven with conscience? Probably both. But I guarantee many people reading this book will find moments when they feel deeply uncomfortable and in that feeling lies hope! But then even hope lies! The next step, of getting it all out in the open, is too much to hope for. It wouldn't be a world any of us recognize.

If you look again at the list of the kinds of lies people tell (chapter 1), you will see that actually people close to each other will indulge in just about all of them. It's a maze to try to sort that out even for the most astute people!

Relationship lies do depend to some extent on expectations. The classic 'open marriage' or marriages of convenience or social mobility, do not in the main contain expectations of fidelity in respect of the partners. If infidelity damages the prospects of the underlying reasons for the marriage (power marriages for example) then those expectations do exist. We won't

Mendacity is a system that we live in. Liquor is one way out and death's the other.
(Tennessee Williams)

even begin to look at those unions where the partners set out to lie to everyone else as a team.

Outside of marriage and oaths given in public, relationships are varied, close and come with the same kinds of stresses and strains and expectations the world over. Today a good deal of cohabiting is, to all intents and purposes, a marriage even to having children, sharing bank accounts and inheritances. And as we begin to understand that it is the bonding, not the mores of society, that are the truly important parts of a relationship we may even begin to see how lies are part of the glue that smooths over troubles, avoids arguments and strengthens the bonds.

Almost everyone will catch a romantic partner in a lie at sometime or other. Even after a small episode the fact of the lie will continue to inform someone of the levels of trust they can place in the other person. These trust issues are unavoidable.

People have a difficult time dealing with the fact that someone close to them has betrayed them. Psychologists often feel that close relationships make the perfect environment for lies. People in a relationship become very intimate, close and vulnerable to each other. They start to believe there is no way their partner could lie to them because they know them so well. This is why lovers lie. It is so easy to do so and in the end they believe it is better than telling the truth if the truth would affect the relationship and/or hurt their partner. We are so used to lying in every situation that we no longer give great importance to what lying is outside of its effect. Deceit has become something we don't actually see in ourselves. We often know when we lie and we often

Please don't lie to me, unless you're absolutely sure I'll never find out the truth.
(Ashleigh Brilliant)

don't even give it a moment's consideration. Only when our lie is found out does it seem to affect us in anyway whatsoever. Some experts suggest that this ingrained habit of lying means the brain does not have to do much thinking about the lies, as suggested earlier. In point of fact they think it far better to concentrate on breaking the habit than analyzing prefontal cortexes.

Time for a list. Here are some of the main issues over which people lie to each other in relationships according to some experts:

Career:

Lovers lie about liking or respecting their partner's job or career. In an age when one's career can define a huge part of who we are this is tantamount to not liking your partner much.

Appearance / Health:

Lovers lie about their age, weight, health, nose job and unexplained holes in their skin.

Attraction to Others:

Lovers lie about their feelings and interest in others especially if they see those people regularly – such as work colleagues. They tend not to lie so much about desiring Hollywood stars but dress up as them in the bedroom.

Someone who knows too much finds it hard not to lie.
(Ludwig Wittgenstein)

Behavior / Character:

Lovers lie about liking their partner's habits, personality, hobbies, sense of humor. (I can't see those relationships lasting long there is nothing worse than marrying a bad comedian).

Beliefs:

Lovers lie about true feelings on important issues like religion, politics, their lover's companion animal, who holds the remote control and who their daughter really looks like.

Betraying Confidences:

Lovers lie to each other about keeping secrets confidential. We love to gossip and when we don't, actually, we make it up anyway.

Career / Performance:

Lovers lie about how well work, school, their career is going, although if it's going very badly this is impossible to conceal from someone who knows your every mood swing. This is also allied to lying about money.

Commitment:

Lovers lie about uncertainty or doubts they are having about the relationship.

I have a higher and grander standard of principle than George Washington. He could not lie; I can, but I wont.
(Mark Twain)

To admit any would start a long, involved argument – something many people want to avoid after a long day spent lying about their income.

Enjoyment:

Lovers lie about enjoying things a partner likes to do. Oh, the misery of fun fairs.

Family / Friends:

Lovers lie about liking other people who are important to a partner such as old friends and even family. None of us can help our relations – so be kind

Feelings:

Lovers lie about their true feelings towards a partner. Especially if the sex is good.

Financial / Issues:

Lovers lie about their income, resources, inheritance, debt and spending habits. Not just because they may be self-conscious about them but because we are taught to conceal our earnings from everyone in case the tax man hears us.

Flirting:

Lovers lie about flirting with strangers and sisters.

If a lie is repeated often enough all the dumb jackasses in the world not only get to believe it, they even swear by it.
(Billy Boy Franklin)

Time with Others:

Lovers hide activities and time spent with others at fun fairs.

Infidelity / Cheating:

Lovers lie about having sex with other people and other people lie about how good it was.

Jealousy:

Lovers lie about being jealous and snooping and why they own packets of latex gloves that don't leave fingerprints

Love / Emotions:

Lovers lie to their partners about feeling vulnerable or scared or deeply moved.

Masturbation:

Men, in particular, lie about masturbating. I mean they lie about when, where, how often – not that they just lie about masturbating!

Past / Relationships:

Lovers lie about the depths of past relationships, as if past feelings are irrelevant to their present relationship.

Make the lie big, make it simple, keep saying it, and eventually they will believe it.
(Adolf Hitler)

Physical Appearance:

Lovers lie about liking their partner's appearance, hair, weight, age, clothes and shoe collection.

Secret Contact:

Lovers lie about intimate, but nonsexual contact with someone else especially if it's an animal

Sexual / Enjoyment:

Lovers lie about how good sex with a partner is. If it is good they don't lie.

Sexual Fantasies:

Lovers conceal having sexual fantasies about others during sex. Or thinking about sex with someone else unless its an agreed role play.

Sexual History:

Lovers lie about the number of past partners, unsafe sex practices, what they have and have not done with others, their virginity, having an abortion, etc.

Sexual / Orientation:

Some lovers lie about same sex contact or interest.

It takes a wise man to handle a lie, a fool had better remain honest.
(Norman Douglas)

Time Management:

Lovers lie about being too busy, or having too much work to do or not having time due to snooping, and flirting, for whatever it is they are expected to be doing.

Of course these are lies within some kinds of normal relationship. There are relationships founded upon lies. Such people who set out to romanticize their own selves or give the relationship a romantic gloss for the sake of the romance, are not uncommon. If you want to be able to recognize such people here are some observations on common romantic relationship lies:

1. Romantic liars are very good at information control. If your partner knows far more about you than you know about them, there's a chance there's a hidden agenda in play. Evading questions about this is also an indicator. You have an idea of what your partner is like, but you've never really had any of the information verified.

2. Romantic liars make you feel like it's love at first sight, because the lying is designed to create intensity and a feeling that you are soaring through the air, in their arms.

3. Romantic liars have a built in need to keep their partners on a short leash and out of contact with people who might know the truth. It is common for romantic liars to go to some rather extraordinary lengths to limit contact with friends, family, co-workers, etc.

4. A lot of romantic liars present themselves as

I believed, therefore have I spoken: I was greatly afflicted: I said in my haste, All men are liars.
(Psalms CXVI)

being more available than they really are.

5. Romantic liars lie about their educational background, their occupation, social connections, and so forth.

6. Romantic liars will often say they have a personal tragedy in their lives, losing a loved one, being in a disaster, etc.

7. Romantic liars will lie about working for the secret service or being a specialist soldier.

8. The internet is a great place for these people!

These people live in a fantasy world created by their own lies. A bit like people who pretend to be lawyers or doctors and apply for jobs in the field. Far from killing the romance, lies can actually give you romance. Even if only for the lifetime of the lies. And most lies do have a lifetime. It's the only good thing to be said for them, in the main the truth will come out. Even if it takes interrogation techniques to get at it or the passing of a hundred years. But then, any lover who has not worked out how to get the truth out of their partner is going to have to live in a cloud of fibs anyway.

Absolute honesty has become something no human beings live with or give. And in close relationships there is an artifice going on, in that a relationship is the creation of two people (or maybe more these days). In that creation there is some moulding going on as we present ourselves to each other at our most vulnerable. Perhaps we should expect that such relationships could actually not exist without a certain amount of lying. Or at least not get started without a certain amount of lying.

Ultimately, it is what we lie about and how

When lying, be emphatic and indignant, thus behaving like your children.
(William Feather)

important those matters are conceived of, by both ourselves and those we love, that matters. Being honest and suggesting someone looks fat (when they do) is very near to an insult and we wouldn't want to insult those we love. On the other hand, lying about having sex with others whilst preventing hurt and the break up of the relationship, does not disguise the fact that actually for at least one person, the relationship is already dead. You would not need to lie about it if fidelity was not an issue.

And I can only imagine what lies are told in polyandrous and polygamous societies. We should give thanks that for the most part, we only have to lie to one person in bed at a time.

Splendide mendax.
Noble Lie
(Horace)

In War And Business
or
The 36 Stratagems

Without lying there would be no wars and business would always be good. War is business by another name and business is war without the bloodshed – although in criminal business one should assume a certain amount of bloodshed.

Business and war even share a language. You can make a killing with a stock, have a tactical meeting to discuss take-overs, martial your defences against a hostile take-over, plan your advertising and growth campaign (propaganda), take out the competition and so forth. In fact business people are probably all would-be generals – loving authority, following a certain discipline; even having an almost world-wide dress code. And if business is a pseudo-war carried out in offices and not on battlefields, and in electronic cyberspace, it is nonetheless true that in both business and war aggression plays a significant role and it is a very sad fact that war, for all the excuses we have for waging them, is and always has been big business.

If money making were taken out of the war machines of the world, and business was not able to subsume other businesses or erode the competition both would be shadows of what they are today in human society. If the great supply-and-demand chain, which

He who tells a lie is not sensible of how great a task he undertakes; for he must be forced to invent twenty more to maintain that one.
(Alexander Pope)

OK LADS, IT'S YOUR JOB
TO MAKE THIS £30 BILLION
DEBT LOOK LIKE A GOOD THING!

hides a million crimes were shackled, civilization itself would be radically different, and in chaining our minds to business we become as single minded and dependent upon those around us as any soldier on any battlefield.

The Chinese thinker and warrior, Sun Tzu ("Master Sun"), also called Sun Wu, is traditionally considered to be the author of The Art of War, an immensely influential ancient Chinese book about military strategy. Strategy is the art of trying to outwit your opponent, an art in which, you can obviously see, lying would play a major

There are a terrible lot of lies going round the world, and the worst of it is that they're true.
(Winston Churchill)

role. This is also one of those areas where lying is usually considered justified because you are saving the lives of the people on 'your side'. However if you take the view, as I do, that countries are artificial constructs and people are the same everywhere, the narrow field of vision which makes warring possible is itself a fabrication which we all plug into. After generations of lies we have become very distrustful, and the putting up of barriers and walls is now second nature to us. This is not to say that we are not sometimes attacked and have to defend ourselves. This is an explanation of the rational that underpins the given reasons for the attack.

In fact Sun Tzu says that all warfare is based on deception and, in waging a war, one should be 'serene and inscrutable' (now those two go together). But before you dismiss him as some oriental thinker not relevant to the 'rest of the world' (and if you did – consider what you mean by world) bear in mind he was studied by Napoleon.

> "In war, force and fraud are the two cardinal virtues."
> (Thomas Hobbes, Leviathan)

All soldiers study the strategy and military campaigns of previous soldiers because there are rules on how to wage a war and prosecute a battle. And note that word 'rules'. It's one of those terms that in context hides an horrific amount, yet appears on the surface to be acceptable. It is acceptable because without some rules war is plain butchery. But even with the rules war is butchery. But the rules fool us. The rules tell us there is some ethical consideration in war. Actually true ethical

The difference between a saint and a hypocrite is that one lies for his religion, the other by it.
(Minna Antrim)

78

considerations would make war the one action we would all work hard to expunge from the future of our endeavours. Except that we have an armaments' trade worth a fortune, practised by powerful countries. What leaders have ever suggested agreements to give that up?

Rules also saturate business. And most of them are there to restrict 'bad' practices and tell business people what practices are allowed and what ones are not. Reminiscent of the long and rather ridiculous arguments Europe had about waging a 'Just War.' Adulterating foods for human consumption saves money and extends profits but is considered unacceptable. Do you think without the rules and the power to back them up, people would never adulterate your food again? Of course they would because, after all, people are not to be trusted.

Business is so ready to lie to us we have to have a plethora of rules and regulations about what they can charge, when they can charge it, and what constitutes a sale of goods and what constitutes a bargain. We have to have safety regulations so that the things we buy in good faith won't kill or maim us, because – when all is said and done – business wants profit. Benefit to the community is secondary and has to be because without profit a business cannot survive. Entire communities can, and have been, sacrificed to the business of profit.

And even with all those laws we still need consumer groups to keep an eye on things. People will sell you things that will poison you if they can make money, and they do in parts of the world we have little interest in extending our safety regulations to. Things business people know kill, harm and poison are sold every day just as soldiers practice every day to kill harm

Falsehood is easy, truth so difficult.
(George Eliot)

and destroy and who knows – even poison.

Wars bring out the bravery and courage in men and women, but it is a fact that much of war is dissembling and falsehood. If it wasn't there would never have been an ambush. In fact only the Scots and Rajputs ever thought ambushes were a silly idea and it was much more to their liking to shout to their enemies and show what big swords they had. An act of true bravery is to go into battle playing bagpipes. It is also a great act of truth because it says we are here and we are coming. Sadly it cannot be said to be 'serene and inscrutable'. Perhaps that is best said of the Gurkhas who fight at night and you don't know they are there until they are cutting off your head. Rather like a hostile business takeover where everything is done very, very fast on all fronts at once in the stock market, with the press and in the lawyers offices to make sure you have the best chance of success.

And after the take over you can dismember the other business and subsume into your structures what you want at your leisure. The legal framework of business empires, and the treaties of olden day Empires are not as different as you may think. In the first place olden day Empires were predicated on the fact that owning more land made a country richer, and the writing of agreements (treaties) and the funneling of profits (trade) works for both.

Money seems to bring out the liar in so many of us one has to ask is it really the money, or just our natures? We hide the true costs to us of things we sell to others, we tell our workers we can't afford what we can afford, our workers try to get benefits without the boss knowing it, we sell things in less regulated countries we cannot sell

A giurar presti i mentitor son sempre. (Liars are always given to swearing.)
(Vittorio Alfieri)

to our own people anymore, knowing it may harm and even kill, we lobby governments, we bribe officials who enjoy the bribes, we even elect crooks to office. And when we have more money than we know what to do with - we run for political power.

Happily, the rich don't lie to us, because they don't even talk to us. They just employ other people to lie to us: "This technology is safe"; "This development is good for you"; "Here is the data, here are test results".

It's all to make money out of us in new ways that have a strangely old feel to them. And worst of all business men and women believe they are doing the right thing for the community because the system is there to be made use of and they are keeping the system sound and in good order. The same system, mark you, that has wiped out thousands of species of animals and hundreds of native peoples running into million of individuals - quite a price to pay for everyone to have a TV set. But I am sure many generals enjoyed it.

Talking about systems, we are told there is no such thing as a free lunch. Actually the correct statement should be: "There is no such thing as a free lunch within the system". The monetary system was not and never has been, natural. There is an argument that war, in as far as it is aggression and counter-aggression, is natural. If true, money is either a way of channeling our aggression so as to create civil society or an unnecessarily aggressive way of creating civilization.

The Earth and everything on it is a free gift – it is human beings who cannot do anything without getting remuneration of some sort. Even the barter system depended upon an idea of mutual benefit. (War of

Lies are usually caused by undue fear of men.
(Chassidic Saying)

course has no such idea unless the combatants are evenly matched and time and losses wear them down until they come to peace talks. Such peace talks are all about mutual benefit if no one has surrendered to convene them).

We are just not that community orientated to work for the joy of it yet funnily enough the whole economic system depends for its existence on the good will of everyone else. We make a small number of people rich simply by living and buying things in bulk. Without the rest of us, and the economic system we all adhere to, there could be no rich people - within the system. I mean you would still have famous people, and leaders and impressive thinkers but there would be no one on Earth who could grow rich by putting a price on originally free, natural resources and selling it to everyone else.

It may be our nature to be unable to build a civilization without money, but money is not natural. And economics being another of those structures with rules and boundaries that we plug into and love so much, enhances the ability we have to lie to ourselves. Many years ago extolling the virtues of Roman and Greek civilization I was told not to be so appreciative of societies that depended upon slave labor. The enslaving and mass slaughter of animals underpins our entire banking system. Not much to extol in that.

Lying about the enemy and to the enemy is important in war. Commonly called propaganda in wartime and advertising in peacetime, it's one and the same thing. Camouflage is the most intelligent way people have ever thought of for saying, "Hey, we're not in!"

It was a fact that in reporting losses and successes

Haven't we mothers all given our sons a taste for lies, lies which from the cradle upwards lull them . . . lies as soft and warm as a breast!
(Georges Bernanos)

in the Battle of Britain the BBC doubled the enemy planes shot down and halved the British Air Force planes shot down. The reason for this was not, as has been suggested,to keep from the population of Britain how dire things really were, but to convince the listening Germans that the British couldn't count. And before you dismiss that as ridiculous, how much respect would you credit an enemy who couldn't count? (It is ridiculous though).

If you don't respect an enemy you will underestimate their intelligence. Lies in war do what they do in peacetime, they confuse and hide true intents and the true nature of things. Lies are a weapon and though we can see this clearly in wartime we should not be blind to the fact that, that is always their purpose. Between individuals they may often be a weapon of defence depending upon the situation and the lie, but they are still a weapon.

Even those lies people agree can be used, to withhold a painful truth from someone, are a weapon being used to defend either the person's feelings or the liar's situation. Aeschylus said that in war, truth is the first casualty. Deception can save your life and often your company (company, another one of those dual words that live in business and war. Engagement is one that lives in relationships and war but I am so not going to look at the similarities between war and relationships, this book isn't long enough.)

Let it be said that as far as deception goes, there are many company directors out there grateful for having creative accountants.

People lie about stocks and shares and what's happening to companies, they spread rumors, they break

Resolved to lie in the last dyke of prevarication.
(Edmund Burke)

the rules, they commit fraud and lie openly; all to take advantage of the ensuing situation and make money. (Rendering unto Caesar what is Caesar's is actually a divine suggestion that you should lie at all times to tax gatherers – and it is heartening how many of us do).

Untangling lies to get at the truth can sometimes feel like a war. Ask any journalist or official receiver.

A business and an army are forms of human community dedicated to different tasks. Like other communities they are based on some assumptions about how people behave within their given task-set: that the community is formed for the benefit of all, that people are working to a common goal as well as to their own individual goals, etc.

Most people treated with honesty and concern will respond with loyalty and hard work. Fear, greed and patriotism can and are used by both these types of community but sometimes in a subtle way. In business, people are taught to fear 'being poor' and have instilled in them that this means being without an income. Is that true poverty? Or is that the definition of poverty within the system?

Lies in the business environment directly benefit the liars, in armies they can save lives which is of benefit to soldiers and generals. Which is ok, if it's your side's lies. Even soldiers know they don't know everything or see the whole picture but they do what they are trained to do as their part in the general effort. Exactly what individuals do in large corporations. Exactly what individuals do inside countries. The wealth of nations is, after all, a description before it becomes an ordinance.

Competitors are often treated as enemy armies are.

To thine own self be true, and it must follow, as the night the day, thou can'st not then be false to any man.
(William Shakespeare)

Good business practice is to gobble up your competition if you can, large corporations are seen as empires, militating against competitors (never give an idiot an even break) are all accepted practice. Why? Because the general public only like to see who is waving the flag and how much wealth/courage they have shown. How many lies have been told to get there is of no interest to them. See how angry people get when foreign owned companies buy their nationally known brands, or when they see people flaunting foreign imported goods. The word 'invasion' is not used much but the feelings generated by global business are much the same.

Perhaps this all reflects the internal war in us all, between truth and lies. Between being honest and telling lies. We wouldn't lie if the situation didn't force us too. We lie either because of our natures or because we are scared of what the truth might do to us. Although this is a comforting thought nonetheless we do take too much delight in some of our lies. And you won't find anywhere in business rules and regulations a simple rule, 'tell the truth all the time.' Business isn't like that.

It is well known that Goebbels used lies as a propaganda weapon. Propaganda is a kind of 'scientific lying'. Its purpose in wartime is to keep everyone in the dark whilst the war is being prosecuted and afterwards to leave such a net of confusion it's impossible to prosecute the generals.

Some argue that all persuasive communication is propaganda, while others suggest that only dishonest messages can be considered propaganda. Lets look at the dishonest side.

Harold Lasswell's broad interpretation of the term.

Telling lies is a fault in a boy, an art in a lover, an accomplishment in a bachelor, and second-nature in a married man.
(Helen Rowland)

"Not bombs nor bread, but words, pictures, songs, parades, and many similar devices are the typical means of making propaganda. . .propaganda relies on symbols to attain its end: the manipulation of collective attitudes."

(H.D. Lasswell, The Theory of Political Propaganda)

Propagandists usually attempt to influence individuals while leading each one to behave "as though (their) response were (their) own decision". Mass communication tools extend the propagandist's reach and make it possible to shape the attitudes of many individuals simultaneously. Because propagandists attempt to "do the other fellow's thinking for him," they prefer indirect messages to overt, logical arguments. We do this by making calculated emotional appeals, by demonizing the enemy, by linking the war to the goals of various social groups, and, when necessary, by lying outright.

Businesses can be tremendously successful without engaging in fraud. While we may be fooled into buying products that are hyped, we also have a special affection for, and often a lifelong relationship to products we like. But all advertising and all propaganda has an angle and it is in that angle, that lies reside.

So effective was the propaganda in World War 2 that people even took against German breeds of dog. Now much as I loathe the Nazis and would see them as my natural enemy, I think it is ridiculous to think someone who owned a Dachshund was somehow unpatriotic. Actually, if they had read this book first, they would have been far more suspicious of people who bought Allied breeds and wrapped themselves up in the flag as if making a public display. The people one would have thought defined Britain, the aristocracy, were

We lie loudest when we lie to ourselves.
(Eric Hoffer)

littered with fascists, and still are.

War and business can appeal to one's emotions, denigrating the other side and appealing to the ends whilst passing over the means. The "War To End All Wars" is not far from, "The only cleaning fluid you will ever need." They are both lies. Objectivity is often difficult. We have employed lies to survive and have sex, to stem arguments and win battles, but now lying can actually limit our ability to reason clearly because we are not getting the information we need to make decisions about our lives. We all need to be far better at recognizing a lie when we are told one.

But that is so difficult when we are taught from an early age, even as our mechanisms for reasoning begin to take shape, to reason within the system.

(I am grateful to Dr.Aaron Delwiche,Associate Professor in the Department of Communication at Trinity University,Texas, for some of these observations).

Ambition drove many men to become false; to have one thought locked in the breast, another ready on the tongue.
(Sallust)

Recognizing a Liar
or
An Um and an Itch

Be careful this chapter may turn you into a conspiracy theorist.

Have we come a long way in the last ninety pages? From seeing how lies start, how they are embedded in our mental abilities, to what extent they are taught and certainly how they are misused. Can we ever stop lying? Could there be a time when we lied 10% of the time, or 5% of the time? Or is the habit, advanced by our natural ability, too ingrained? Perhaps we could, if we started to call each other out more when we hear a lie, but to do that we need to be sure. Sure that we are being lied to and sure that we don't mind having no friends!

Before you read this chapter you should have some idea in your mind of what kind of lies you want to know about and what kind you are indifferent to. If your best friend when asked what they did last night and instead of saying they were in place 'a' they say there were in place 'b' do you really care that much? You make the rules for your life. Of course if your girlfriend was in place 'a' it may make all the difference in the world.

It is impossible to always detect a lie but you can limit the odds. The work that has been done amongst jurors seems to show that contrary to popular belief, women are not much better at judging when someone is lying than men. According to those trained in the police

If one is to be called a liar, one may as well make an effort to deserve the name.
(A. A. Milne)

HOW MUCH WOOD WOULD A WOODCHUCK CHUCK,
IF A WOODCHUCK COULD CHUCK WOOD?

services about 4% of people are accomplished liars and they can lie very well.

In the following list please note if you are going to do jury service, don't pay the items any attention. You will not be conversant with a body language that is culturally different from what you were brought up to understand and potential indicators of lying are also indicators of natural stress, illnesses and psychological problems. I wouldn't want you to find the innocent guilty because of this little book.

All lies and jests, still a man hears what he wants to hear and disregards the rest.
(Paul Simon)

Liars are not just poker-faced, they are as expressionless as humanly possible (if they are not people simply suffering from Möbius syndrome.) Bland and restricted they move their arms and hands rarely and when they do, movements tend to be inwards, towards their own bodies, as if they were trying to take up less space than usual. Few liars are effusive in their lies. What movements there are may be are off-timed and inappropriate (frowning at a piece of whimsy, smiling at a serious rejoinder, for example.)

Liars nearly always avoid eye contact. Even introverted people will glance into your eyes once in a while whilst talking to you, painfully shy people will look down, but liars actively avoid eye contact and look down and blink less (some sociologists say this is a misconception as lies are so habituated the liars don't even think about them as lies so are not abashed at using them.)

Liars will touch their face, throat and mouth as they talk. They will scratch their nose and/or behind their ear. Remember they may do this even when they have told the lie and stopped talking. The lie 'lives' while the conversation continues. It also comes back to haunt them – we hope.

Liars will change the pitch of voice or rate of speech (this can also be a sign of singing).

Liars displays of emotion may be delayed and when they arrive, stay longer than natural.

Liars are the cause of all the sins and crimes in the world.
(Epictetus)

Liars very often preface everything they say with an exaggerated, "Uh. . . ." Beware of the person who responds to every one of your queries with "Uh". Men do this more than women. (Uh, um – how many politicians have you heard doing that?) This will be especially true of most lies as they are given 'in the moment' and off the cuff. Practised liars with their planned lies will be fluent. So in effect politicians who 'um' a lot are not practised liars. How comforting.

A liar gets defensive if challenged. An innocent person will often go on the offensive. In fact, challenging someone you think has lied is often a good way of proving it. Taking them by surprise will make them have to say something more rapidly than they can think it out. The unexpected questions, as interrogators term them.

A liar is uncomfortable facing the person they are lying to. If they are lying to a lot of people at once this is shown by the fact they look around the room not catching anyone's eye, and even turn their body away. This should not be confused with teaching.

Liars might unconsciously place objects (book, coffee cup, etc.) between themselves and you. This is part of their instinctive defence but it does rely on how serious they consider their lie to be. Saying your phone was out of order when you didn't pick up, might not be a big lie. Saying you paid with a larger amount of money than you actually did, so the retailer gives more change might be seen as a big lie, in which case an entire

Lying is done with words and also with silence.
(Adrienne Rich)

counter is placed between the two of you as a cup would not be sufficient!

A liar will mirror your own words to answer to a question. When asked, "Did you eat the last cookie?" The liar answers, "No, I did not eat the last cookie". It's almost as if they are learning to speak your language.

A liar wants to go. They may end the conversation unexpectedly and lie about why!

A statement with a contraction is more likely to be truthful: "I didn't do it" instead of "I did not do it". A liar tries to be subtly emphatic. If you think the liar is convinced of the truth of their statement, you are more likely to believe in it. This goes wider into the 'use' of language as it is perfectly true that good orators know many tricks and people untrained in oratory can be carried away by the sentiments and use of language and barely see the wider picture. Impressive dictators usually have excellent oratorical skills. Their ability to tell the truth (if they have it) is often less well practised and less needed.

Liars may not make direct statements. Their answers may be implied so you cannot come back at them with their own words later and tell them they are cheap. They can respond that you misunderstood them and there was no lie given. Many years ago I went to hire a room in a college of which I was not a member and the Don asked me, "Are you a student here?" I knew he meant of the college but I took it in my apology two

A truth that's told with bad intent beats all the lies you can invent.
(William Blake)

days later, that he meant the University itself (when you study linguistic logic this kind of dualism in meaning in common-place.) He accepted my apology and for my lie I didn't get to hire the room. We still had the party.

Liars can be garrulous, adding unnecessary details to convince you, they are simply not comfortable with a silence or pause in the conversation. Maybe because they don't want you to have the time to figure out what they have said is a lie. Since most lies are given at the spur of the moment, sometimes for unthought-out reasons and reasons even the liar cannot explain except maybe to keep in practice, they are unsure of the logic and whether it all hangs together. Liars want the conversation to be well and truly over.

However, bear in mind, an excellent liar adds effective details. Anyone who watches Kevin Spacey's brilliant near-last scene in The Usual Suspects will understand how persuasive this can be. This takes a high level of intellect and it is a fact that more intelligent people can lie effectively to less intelligent people. They can also talk down to them which is annoying because it is not a sign of intelligence at all.

A liar may leave out pronouns and speak in a monotonous tone. When a truthful statement is made the pronoun is emphasized as much or more than the rest of the words in a statement. I simply don't know what comments I can make about this. If it is true, then some very small words in English have the same affect as sodium thiopental. At least that is what I intend to

It is easier to believe a lie that one has heard a thousand times than to believe a fact that no one has heard before.
(Anonymous)

tell anyone who suggests I need interrogating before they allow me into the United Sates for my book tour.

A liar's words may be garbled and spoken softly, and syntax and grammar may be off. In other words sentences will likely be muddled rather than emphasized. A bit like telling a story as you go. This of course is most pronounced in a lie that is quite long. Which is why we like our lies to be short and swift, like our affairs. If you have a gut reaction that you are being lied to, you might be picking up on micro-expressions which last about a 25th of a second but are indicative of a concealed emotion. These are the same kinds of expression as normal, frowns, smiles etc. but so fast the eye barely picks them up but the brain nonetheless registers their passing.

Making contradictory statements that just don't hold together should make you suspicious someone is lying (or drunk).

Look for inconsistencies with the way things usually are. The world works in a certain way and oddities should be taken into account – except in England, home to great eccentricities, where oddities should be taken with a pinch of salt. You want to pay attention to someone who is generally anxious, but now appears calm or vice-versa. This supposes that you know the liar quite well. Amongst those who train liars (yes, they exist) having as little contact with your victim (the lyee – and I am so hoping this new word does not get into the language) is recommended for this very reason.

Lying is an indispensable part of making life tolerable.
(Bergen Evans)

You would think relationship lies could not happen as much as they do if familiarity breeds perception. Perhaps, as we noted above, we deliberately give people we know more rope because we don't want to believe they could lie to us.

Liars take advantage of the situation. It will be easier to lie in an e-mail than face-face. It will be easier to lie in passing than in a long, drawn out conversation. It will be easier to lie if you are strangers. Situations in which you know lies ensure may be: have you just arrested them? Are they appearing as witnesses for the Defence? Are they your lawyer? Are they selling you something?

Low self-esteem, depression and drug addictions are associated with compulsive lying. So you should show compassion to these liars but not weakness.

Now remember a good actor is supposed to be able do the overwhelming majority of the things on that list with conviction. If you recall the chapter on children you will remember that all lies are told to manipulate a situation in the liar's favour, or at least to the disadvantage of those being lied to. So one question you could always ask yourself if you suspect you are being lied to is; who benefits from my believing this? It is a very useful question.

Most thinkers who have approached the topic of lying tend to think some lies worse than others (those saints again) and the situation in which the lie is given is a mitigating factor. We read an impartial, incomplete list

You lie--under a mistake-- for this is the most civil sort of lie that can be given to a man's face, I now say what I think.
(Pedro Calderon de la Barca)

in chapter one. Taking this a stage further experts have concocted a list of the types of liar. Within any circle of friends when you gossip about each other I am sure you will have come across these kinds of liars:

Delusional:

These people want their lies to be the truth (a lot of charlatan practices fit this category). They are mostly lies about their circumstances or background or position in their workplace.

Fibbers:

I am including a category for those people whom we don't want to call liars. Usually aunts. They have wonderful stories and inventions but they never mean to harm anyone, anytime, anywhere.

Frequent:

The other end of the scale. They are not uncomfortable lying but because they do it a lot they often make mistakes in their sequence of events within which they have couched their lie (or maybe they are drunk a lot).

Habitual:

Habitual liars are fairly uncommon, at least in the United Kingdom. These are people who have difficulty separating fact

Dare to be true: nothing can need a lie; A fault which needs it most, grows two thereby.
(George Herbert)

from fiction. But catching them out is like shooting fish in a barrel and depends only on whether you feel it is worth your time. For them it's just a hobby.

Occasional:

This is most of us and this is where we fidget most. We do this to avoid any unpleasantness, we don't lie a lot, we don't even like lying, but yet we do. It is not impossible some of them will be big lies but for the most part they are probably small lies.

Popular and Unpopular:

Some people we enjoy lying to us. Storytellers, magicians and other entertainers who fool us with their work. Some we don't enjoy but we still let go like politicians who end up with titles and immense wealth for a life-time of evasion (and sometimes invasion).

Professional:

These people plan the details of their lies and even rehearse answers if you catch them out on a particular statement. They want their lies to work and will refine them by using them on different people until they work well. They not only include people selling you something, they

Repetition does not transform a lie into a truth.
(Franklin D. Roosevelt)

also include con-artists and crooks and 'modern' art.

Sociopaths:

Of course these people will lie. They are manipulative, often quite callous, shallow, lacking in guilt with a tendency to criminality to lesser or greater degrees and often have an inflated opinion of their own worth especially when set against the worth of another individual. Probably you dated someone like this at some time in your life.

In every generation we have tried to catch out lies, some great, some smaller, some huge. Some history has been made because of lies and some lies are lost in the mists of time.

Indeed if a lie comes to be believed, it has all the hallmarks of truth so does it really matter any more if it is false as we cannot prove it one way or the other? We still base a lot of our civilized expectations on thousand year old assumptions that were made by men and woman who did not have the same view or knowledge of the universe we have today. And in a hundred years that knowledge will be even greater if we are all still here, and who is to say our assumptions today will not appear absurd to our great grandchildren?

How many people still believe animals have no languages or feelings? How many people go out with precision guns and shoot herbivores from cover and call

Believe those who are seeking the truth. Doubt those who find it.
(Andre Gide)

themselves hunters instead of killers? How many people believe a city to be a great monument to human design instead of a breeding places for disease and, in effect, a giant bank? And how many of us still believe nature is to be conquered more than loved? So many of the lies we live by have come from ancient people who believed them to be true, we have no such excuse. We have come to lie so readily we have begun to believe our own lies. At the very least its great material for cartoonists.

If we have a natural ability to lie it is still true that we are taught how to use it. However, those first lies which we use as children to help and which have no malicious intent, become malicious as we grow up. We use lies to protect ourselves and when we are protecting ourselves from harm or death it is considered just. But an ability that is 'just' in extreme cases, like so many of our abilities, crosses different lines in our view of ethics when we use them in casual, everyday circumstances. We have come to the place where some thinkers suggest if we started telling the truth, civil society would break down in a single day.

The question arises again and again as to why we accept being lied to by those around us: by advertisers, by politicians, by business people, by those we love? And we do accept it and what is more we lie back. It is true enough that lying has helped us survive against an antagonistic world and even worse, antagonistic people, but what helped one million people survive in a single city two thousand years ago, has become ingrained in our global, six billion large civilization.

We are at that point in our global civilization, everyone reaches in their own relationships, when lying

The opposite of a correct statement is a false statement. But the opposite of a profound truth may well be another profound truth.
(Niels Bohr)

is detrimental to the survival of that relationship.

We are actually at the point where truth will save us. Where honesty will breach our natures and marry our reason to our values. There is nothing stopping us being more transparent except some residue fear that somehow being honest makes us vulnerable.

We have spent some time looking at politics, relationships and warfare and business. Its an eclectic mix. We could have chosen other spheres such as education and medicine. In medicine the noble lie is most profound because it is here that time and again lying to someone who is dying to save them pain, or stem a suicide attempt, is repeated by ethicists down the generations as being an ok lie. However if the patient is also a doctor it is useless to lie to them because they know what you know.

And if you come away from this book with a smile and nothing else remember that lesson. If you have as much knowledge as the liar you cannot be lied to. Knowledge is your path to truth. Liars depend upon your ignorance.

And that little bit of wisdom is worth remembering.

Almost the End

Men occasionally stumble over the truth, but most of them pick themselves up and hurry off as if nothing ever happened.
(Sir Winston Churchill)

NOW BE HONEST... YOU WEREN'T ENTIRELY TRUTHFUL IN YOUR PERSONAL ADD WERE YOU!

As one knows the poet by his fine music, so one can recognize the liar by his rich rhythmic utterance, and in neither case will the casual inspiration of the moment suffice. Here, as elsewhere, practice must precede perfection.
(Oscar Wilde)

THE END